Handmade Style: Japan

Handmade Style

Japan

by Dorothy Wood

Photographs by Lucy Mason

CHRONICLE BOOKS

SAN FRANCISCO

First published in the United States in 2000 by Chronicle Books.

Library of Congress Cataloging-in-Publication Data available.

ISBN 0-8118-2814-X

Printed in Italy

Distributed in Canada by Raincoast Books
8680 Cambie Street
Vancouver, British Columbia V6P 6M9

10 9 8 7 6 5 4 3 2 1

Chronicle Books
85 Second Street
San Francisco, California 94105

www.chroniclebooks.com

contents

introduction

Today's Japanese culture is defined by rules and conventions that have been handed down from generation to generation. Such time-honored practices as removing shoes before entering the house and ritual hot baths are as essential a part of modern Japanese life as are low tables for eating, futons for sleeping, and *tatami* mats. Other unique aspects that typify Japan, such as the kimono, *shoji* paper screens, and simple, exquisite gardens, are instantly recognizable, but it is the interpretation of these elements that allows us to create the style in our own homes.

The Japanese way of life differs in many fundamental ways from that in the West, but the void between the two cultures is narrowing as modern life begins to mingle with traditional values. Indeed, modern technology is as omnipresent in the Japanese home as it is elsewhere. One of the principal differences between East and West is in the layout of rooms in the house. In the West, rooms are generally furnished for a single purpose, and when not in use become "dead" spaces. By contrast, only the kitchen and bathroom are defined in Japanese homes—other rooms are multi-purpose and can be used for living, eating, or sleeping. Adaptable layouts, simple movable furniture, and bedding that can be rolled up

and stored during the day combine to allow an enviable amount of flexibility. Indeed, the traditional Japanese home appears to be almost completely devoid of furniture: a typical room would have nothing more than a few floor cushions and the occasional chest. It is this simplicity and functionalism that has such universal appeal.

In reality, even in the traditional Japanese home, lack of space and the paraphernalia of modern life prevents all rooms from being beautiful and minimalist. Rather than attempting to recreate the perfect Japanese room, I have chosen to impart a little of this unique style into the home with a selection of

INTRODUCTION

beautiful things. The projects are grouped into five chapters according to the material that they are made from: fabric, reed and cane, paper, wood and stone, and bamboo. There are accessories and furniture to add a little Japanese style to every room in the house. The bathroom is the best place to begin: its uncluttered appearance is the ideal backdrop for one or two stunning accessories. Soft white towels hung on a bamboo towel rail with a kimono instantly add a touch of the East when displayed with a simple soap dish or cedar bath mat. In the living room, keep the furnishings low with a few scattered floor cushions and a subtle, elegant paper floor lamp, then choose between a glass and bamboo table or the classic raffia-covered footstool for your coffee cups or tea tray. A traditional folding reed screen makes a stunning focal point when set in one corner, but can be brought out to separate off an eating area. In Japan, the presentation of food is seen as an art form. Great pains are taken when entertaining guests to make sure that everything from the food to the table setting is perfect. The beautiful *sashiko* table mats look elegant on the dinner table, and you can surprise your guests by presenting some pretty Japanese crackers on a stunning rattan tray. To end the meal, serve tea in an elegant teapot on a beautiful lacquered tea tray.

The hallway is usually a forgotten area in the house where people dump their bags and take off their shoes. Ideally the entrance to the home should be an attractive, welcoming area that sets the tone for the rest of the house. You can brighten the area with a bold and colorful door curtain, and then arrange the household's shoes on a sturdy bamboo shoe rack. If there is room for a small table, create a simple *ikebana* arrangement in a pair of tall paper vases.

Lighting is an essential component of the Japanese style. Hang beautiful translucent blinds on the

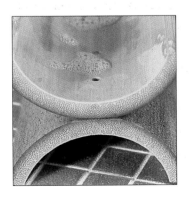

window to filter the sunlight, and choose a paper-covered lamp to soften any existing harsh lighting at night. In the evening, light a stone candle holder on the patio so that you can enjoy the peace and serenity of the garden by soft candle-light. Or you can bring the plants indoors—the water garden in this book is a miniaturized version of a real Japanese garden, with lush foliage, pretty stones, and a wonderful bubbling fountain.

putting it together

I have a great belief that anybody who is "good with their hands" can use their skills to make things using different materials. After all, whether working with wood, bamboo, or fabric, many of the same skills, such as marking, measuring, and cutting, apply. The only difference is the choice of tool. In order to get the best results in any craft you will need to use the right tool for the job. Choosing the best quality is never a wasted investment, as you will inevitably find further use for a good tool. The miter saw, essential for making the angled joints on the reed screen, also cuts straight and is ideal for cutting sections of bamboo. The bamboo can be clamped securely and the saw is guided throughout to allow even the least experienced person to make a perfect clean cut. Wider pieces of wood for the water garden and tea tray can be cut to size at the local lumber yard. Surprisingly, no screws were used to

make any of the projects: the soap dish is held together with bamboo skewers, and the water garden base is simply glued. Accurate measuring is required before drilling the holes for the towel rail. To get a snug fit, make the hole slightly smaller and open out carefully with a round file.

The fabric projects require basic sewing machine skills and are very easy to construct because most of the stitching involved is in straight lines. The traditional Japanese techniques included in this book, such as appliqué and quilting, are quite easy to learn as they require only basic hand stitches such as running stitch and slip hemming. The success of these projects relies on the careful choice of fabrics to create an authentic Japanese look.

As with all crafts, accuracy is the key to a professional result. Both the cane frame for the paper lamp and the paper blind require precise measuring and cutting. To make it almost foolproof, the design for the paper blind is scaled up and used as a giant template to guide you through each stage. A lesser degree of skill is required for the papier mâché bowls and tall vases: these are simple enough even for a child to make.

Whatever your ability, there is something for everyone in this varied selection of projects. Using natural materials with originality and sensitivity to make simple, functional furnishings and accessories is the essence of Japanese craftsmanship and the means to creating the style.

fabric

▶ 11

Textiles are one of the most exciting aspects of Japanese culture. Traditionally used for clothing such as kimonos and *obis*, the fabrics are a rich resource for use in interior design. By using authentic fabrics or modern prints it is quite easy to add a little Japanese style to your home. You can make the kimono-inspired bolster cushion or cover a couple of floor cushions in a matter of hours. The floor cushions are smaller and flatter than the ones you might be used to, but they can be stacked for extra height and comfort.

Fabrics are imported from Japan either by the yard (meter) or as finished garments. I used a beautiful second-hand silk crêpe kimono for the bodies of the fish on the door curtain. Unlike Western clothing, the kimono is made from a number of simple rectangles and can easily be dismantled and reused. The kimono used in this project had been stitched entirely by hand and was made from long rectangles, each 8in (20cm) wide. Its striking chrysanthe-mum pattern was chosen simply because the design of the gilded petals looked like fish scales, and the red print matched the back-ground *azumino* cotton exactly. The door curtain can be made to fit any size of door by adding extra panels and continuing the design—or you could use it for a window or simply as a wall hanging. Soft, traditional *azumino* fabric is ideal for sitting on and always looks good because it already has natural creases. Both the floor cushions and the table mats use indigo dyed prints to contrast with the plain *azumino* fabric. In keeping with Japanese technique, I chose a delicate butterfly print for the binding on the tablemats to contrast with the sharp, geometric *sashiko* quilting used on the main panels.

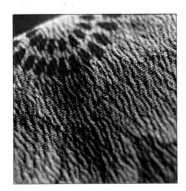

FABRIC

sashiko
table mats

These elegant table mats are made from a traditional Japanese fabric called *azumino*. It was originally used to make sturdy garments for people who worked outside. This heavy cotton fabric is most commonly dyed a dark indigo blue, and has a loose weave that facilitates quilting. Originally, two layers of *azumino* fabric were held together with simple running stitches for extra warmth. The rough stitches were purely functional to begin with, but over the years became increasingly decorative. The stitching is known as *sashiko*, pronounced "sah-sh-ko." The word is often mispronounced: it should be a soft-sounding word with similar emphasis placed on each syllable. *Sashiko* differs from traditional Western quilting in that the thread is coarser and more prominent, and so the stitching itself becomes a major feature of the finished piece. These table mats have a thin layer of cotton batting to protect the tabletop from hot plates, and are bound with a contrasting indigo print.

► 15

The diamond pattern used for the *sashiko* quilting is an ancient Chinese design that has become popular in Japan because it looks like the bark of the indigenous pine tree.

Practice working the *sashiko* quilting on spare pieces of fabric and batting until you can make the stitches an even size. Traditionally there are between five and seven stitches per inch. If you can't find traditional *sashiko* thread in your craft store, use thick embroidery thread.

16 ◄

BASIC SEWING SKILLS REQUIRED

MATERIALS
(TO MAKE FOUR MATS)
◆ *1yd/1m dark indigo* azumino *fabric*
◆ *²⁄₃yd/0.5m thin cotton batting*
◆ *Tracing paper*
◆ *Dressmaker's chalk*
◆ *Dressmaker's carbon paper*
◆ *Tracing wheel*
◆ *Basting thread*
◆ *Medium thickness* sashiko *thread or coton à broder*
◆ *²⁄₃yd/0.5m patterned fabric*
◆ *Sewing kit and sewing machine*

Finished size of each mat:
10½ x 16½in/27 x 42cm

The mats are made from traditional Japanese *azumino* **fabric bound at the edges by a pretty contrasting print.**

1 Cut out eight pieces of 10 x 16in/25 x 40cm plain *azumino* fabric. Here we used a deep indigo color. Cut four pieces of batting to a slightly larger size.

2 Trace the *sashiko* pattern on page 107 onto several pieces of tracing paper and tape the pieces together accurately to make a pattern which is large enough to cover the whole area of the table-mat fabric.

3 Fold a piece of fabric into four and mark its middle point with dressmaker's chalk. Unfold and lay the carbon paper face down on the right side of the fabric. Position the tracing paper pattern on top, making sure that the middle of a diamond is positioned in the previously marked middle point and checking that the pattern is centered on the mat. *(see picture next column)*

4 Draw along the lines with a pencil or use a tracing wheel to transfer the pattern to the fabric.

5 Layer two of the fabric pieces with the batting in the middle and the marked fabric on top. Baste through all the layers using long basting stitches radiating out from the center.

6 Using the *sashiko* thread, work running stitches along the marked lines to quilt the layers.

7 Try to keep the stitches and spaces an even size on the top fabric—the reverse side is not so important and these stitches will probably look like a row of dots. To retain the traditional look, avoid letting any stitches meet at the points of the diamonds. (*see picture right*)

8 Cut the contrasting patterned fabric into bias strips 1 ¼in/3cm wide.

9 Join the strips together, on the diagonal, until you have made one strip long enough to fit around the edge of the mat.

10 Press the seams on the binding strip flat and the long sides under ¼in/6mm.

11 Trim the corners of the mats to a soft curve. Open out one side of the bias strip and pin it around the edges of the mat with right sides together.

12 Mark the places where the ends of the bias binding overlap and join with a diagonal seam.

13 Baste and machine stitch the bias binding along the fold line ¼in/6mm in from the raw edge. Fold to the reverse side and pin to the edges of the mat.

14 Carefully hem the binding to the machine stitches, making sure your stitches are even and neat. (*see picture at right*)

15 Press the table mats lightly on the reverse side before using. Because they are made from an indigo-dyed fabric which will run, it is preferable to wash the mats separately by hand with a mild detergent, and leave to dry naturally. Do not tumble dry.

bolster cushion

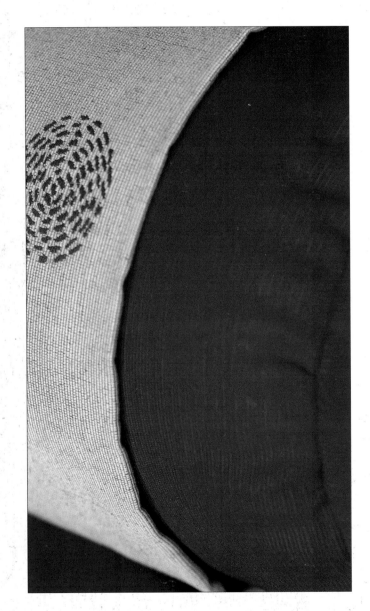

With space at a premium in the majority of Japanese homes, futons and quilts are usually stored in cupboards when not in use. In the traditional home, futons are set out at night on the thick straw *tatami* mats used for flooring and made up with a goose-feather duvet and pillow. At other times the futon can be laid out with cushions and a bolster as a day bed. If the day bed is positioned near a window or on the veranda you can enjoy a view of the garden while reading a book or taking a peaceful nap.

A bolster cushion is the ideal shape to fit across a narrow futon or at the end of a sofa. It is made with a flat end to fit against the back of the sofa or against a wall. The bolster is very simply made from a tube of fabric with a deep bound edge and finished with a thick padded band. The decorative band is styled on the *obi* sash traditionally worn around the waist with a kimono. You can tie a real *obi* sash around a plain cushion to achieve a similar effect.

The printed concentric circle pattern on the cushion's *obi* sash has been cleverly designed to look like simple *sashiko* quilting. If your fabric is plain, use a thick embroidery thread to stitch the pattern.

This style of cushion has a flat end so it will fit into the back of a sofa as an arm rest. Alternatively, it can be made with a knot at each end to be used as a day pillow on a futon or bed.

MATERIALS

- *1yd/1m plain fabric*
- *18in/45cm long, 8in/20cm diameter bolster cushion pad*
- *Dressmaker's chalk*
- *½yd/½m contrasting patterned fabric*
- *30in/76cm strip compressed batting*
- *Sewing kit and sewing machine*

Finished size: 18 x 8in/45 x 20cm

1 Cut the plain fabric to fit the pad, 26in x 1yd/66cm x 1m. Place the long edges together with wrong sides facing. Stitch ⅜in/1cm from the edge.

2 Trim the seam allowance to ⅛in/3mm and press open. Turn the tube through to the reverse side and press the seam flat. Machine stitch ¼in/5mm from the edge to make a French seam.

3 Machine two rows of gathering stitch around one end of the tube. Gathering stitch is a large straight machine stitch with the top tension loosened slightly so that the thread can be pulled up to gather the fabric.

4 Measure the diameter of the bolster cushion pad and cut a circle of the plain fabric to exactly the same size. Mark both the ends of the tube and the circle of fabric in quarters with dressmaker's chalk and then pin in position, matching the marks as you go. Ease the gathers until the circle fits. Machine stitch ⅝in/1.5cm from the edge.

5 For the binding at the opposite end of the cushion, cut out a piece of the contrasting fabric 6in/15cm deep and long enough to fit around the tube, adding 1¼in/3cm seam allowance. Machine stitch the two short ends together and press the seam open. Pin, with right sides together, to the end of the fabric tube. Machine stitch and fold the facing in half. Turn under the raw edge and hem on the inside to the machine stitches. *(see picture next column)*

6 Insert the cushion pad and tie the loose end of the fabric in a knot. *(see picture opposite)*

7 Cut a 14 x 26in/36 x 66cm piece of the contrasting fabric for the *obi* sash on the outside of the cushion, making sure that the pattern is positioned centrally along the length of the sash. Stitch the two long edges together. Press the seam open and turn through, keeping the seam in the center.

8 Cut a piece of batting to fit inside the *obi* sash, and insert it. Wrap the padded *obi* around the bolster cushion and pin the back seam. Tuck one end inside the other and slip stitch securely.

FABRIC

appliquéd curtain

Japan is an intensely visual nation. Walking down a typical shopping street there is a myriad of textures and surfaces to be seen. Produce is beautifully arranged in the street markets, and shops often have a striking *noren* or curtain across the doorway.

These heavy curtains are cleverly designed with split panels so that the customers can walk through into the shop without having to pull the curtain to one side. *Noren* can be quite wide, made up with as many as eight panels.

Because of their size, the design and color of the *noren* are usually quite bold. The giant fish swimming across this curtain were inspired by the carp-shaped windsocks (*koinobori*) that flutter from long poles during the Boy's Day festival held each year on May 5. According to Japanese mythology, the carp is brave and strong, qualities that are vital for a young boy entering a man's world. In Japanese culture the use of particular colors also has deep symbolic implications. Red is considered to be a masculine color, associated with good fortune, and is said to create a positive environment for decision-making.

▶ 23

An old silk kimono was carefully taken apart to provide the fabric for the fish. The chrysanthemum pattern was chosen because the petals have a similar shape to fish scales.

It is crucial that the proportions of this curtain are correct.
For a typical 79in-/2m-high doorway, each panel should be no narrower than 16in/40cm.
The curtain shown here has three 16in/40cm panels.

BASIC SEWING SKILLS REQUIRED

MATERIALS
- *Lining wallpaper*
- *Pencil and ruler*
- *Thick fiber-tipped pen*
- *2⅞yd/2.5m red azumino fabric*
- *Dressmaker's carbon paper*
- *Tracing wheel*
- *1yd/1m contrasting, patterned fabric for appliqué*
- *Sewing kit and sewing machine*
- *2yd/2m cotton sateen lining fabric*

Finished size: 48 x 79in/120 x 200cm

1 Decide on the width and height of the door curtain and divide the width by three to find the size of the panels.

2 Mark out the curtain onto long strips of lining paper. Divide into 4in/10cm squares to match the template on page 108 at the back of the book.

3 Scale up the template by transferring the design onto the paper with a pencil, square by square. Once you are happy

with the design, draw over the lines with a thick fiber-tipped pen.

4 Cut out the panels from the *azumino* fabric, allowing a 2in/5cm seam allowance all around.

5 Lay the fabric panels out on a clean surface and position the lining paper with the enlarged design on top. Slip the dressmaker's carbon under the first section and pin to hold it in place.

6 Run the tracing wheel along the marked lines. Keep the dressmaker's carbon moving until the entire design has been transferred.

7 Carefully tear along the perforations and pin the fish-pattern pieces to the contrasting fabric that you are using for the appliqué. If the fabric's pattern is quite prominent, make sure it is matched across the panels.

8 Cut out the appliqué pieces for the fishes' bodies with a ¼in/6mm seam allowance along the top and bottom

edges and 1in/2.5cm at the sides. Pin the appliqué pieces in position onto the main fabric panels. Turn the edges under along the marked lines and pin. Leave the raw fabric edges along the "gill line" and also at the side edges.

9 Slip stitch the turned-under edges and work running stitch along the raw edges.

10 Cut out the fishes' heads with a ¼in/6mm seam allowance all around. Pin and slip stitch along the lines.

11 You can use the fabric's pattern to make effective fishes' eyes. Here I used the centers of the flowers.

JAPAN

12 To make the eyes, cut out circles from the printed fabric with a ¼in/6mm seam allowance. Turn the raw edges under and baste around the circle carefully. Pin and slip stitch to the fish heads.

13 On the curtain, pin and stitch the seams 10in/25cm down from the top. Cut three 11in/28cm facing panels from the *azumino* fabric to the same width as the curtains, and stitch the seams. Cut out seven 7 x 16in/18 x 40cm tabs for the curtain to hang from.

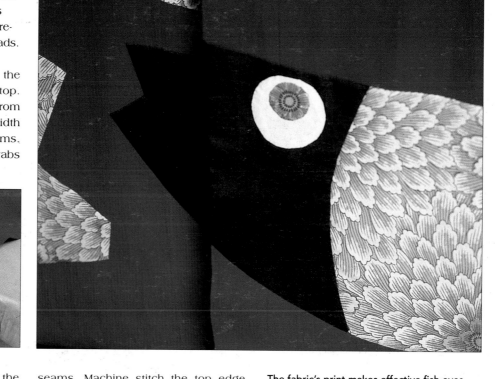

14 On each tab, machine stitch the seams lengthways, press open, and turn through. Position the seams in the center and press flat.

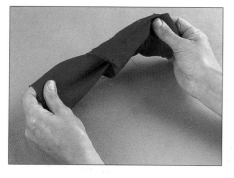

15 Fold the tabs in half and pin, equally spaced, along the top edge of the curtain. Pin the facing on top, matching the seams. Machine stitch the top edge. Trim the seams within the facing to reduce bulk, then fold the facing over to the reverse side and pin in position.

16 Press the side seams and cut and fold diagonally across the bottom corners of the curtain panels to miter them.

The fabric's print makes effective fish eyes.

17 Cut the lining fabric to the same width as the pressed panels and long enough to tuck under the facing. Turn under 1in/2.5cm around the edges and press. Pin and slip stitch the lining and facing to complete the curtain.

FABRIC

floor
cushions

In comparison with their Western equivalent, Japanese homes are sparsely furnished. The high cost of real estate in Japan means that space is at a premium and rooms often double up as areas for eating and sleeping. Furniture is therefore less substantial and infinitely more movable and adaptable. Instead of chairs, floor cushions, known as *zabuton*, are the norm, as they can be neatly stacked to one side ready for the futon to be unrolled at bedtime.

Textiles are perhaps one of the greatest treasures of Japanese handicrafts. The traditional folk fabrics, usually indigo-dyed with an off-white print, have a dynamism and spontaneity that is unparalleled in the West. These beautiful prints have a story behind them: according to legend, the angry sun goddess plunged the world into darkness by hiding in her cave. Other spirits enticed her out by waving blue and white fabric banners outside the cave.

These modern cushions combine an indigo print fabric with plain *azumino* cotton. If you can't find authentic *azumino*, you can use any plain, loose-weave cotton fabric. The cushions are finished with ornate tassels similar to those traditionally used—with hooks—for bamboo blinds.

Exquisite Turk's head knotted tassels pick up the pale beige color of the print and add a stunning finishing touch to these floor cushions.

If you use feather-filled cushion pads, cover them with a feather-proof calico fabric, which prevents feathers from working through to the surface when you sit on the cushions.

BASIC SEWING SKILLS REQUIRED

MATERIALS
(TO MAKE ONE CUSHION)
- *22in/55cm cushion pad*
- *30in/75cm plain azumino fabric 1½yd/140cm wide*
- *13in/34cm square patterned fabric*
- *Small sheet thick card*
- *Size 20 crochet thread*
- *3yd/3m of ⅛in/3mm cord*
- *Sewing kit and sewing machine*

Finished size: 22 x 22in/55 x 55cm

1 For the back panel, cut out a 30 x 23in/77 x 58cm piece across the width of the plain *azumino* fabric. From the same fabric, cut four 6 x 23in/15 x 58cm strips with the grain facing in the same direction as the first piece.

2 Fold a hem of ¾in/2cm across each of the back panel's shorter edges, and machine stitch.

3 Cut the back panel into two pieces across its width, 9in/23cm from one end. This will form the opening for the cushion.

4 Place two of the plain *azumino* strips together with their right sides facing. Fold over the top corner of the fabric onto the other strip at an angle of 45 degrees and press the resulting fold. Pin and machine stitch along the fold line, stopping ⅝in/1.5cm from the inside edge. (*see picture next column*)

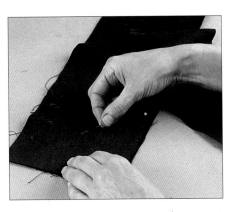

5 Join the other strips together in the same way to create a square border. Trim the diagonal seam allowances to ⅝in/1.5cm and press open.

6 Turn under the seam allowance to ⅝in/1.5cm around the inside of the border and press.

7 Position the panel of contrasting fabric behind the border and adjust until the pattern fits centrally inside the "window." Pin and machine stitch close to the edge.

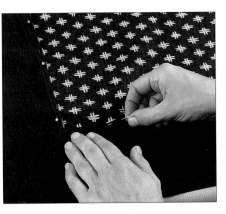

8 Lay the front panel face down and pin the narrower part of the back panel along one of its edges. Pin the larger part of the back panel to the opposite side of the front panel. Pin the sides together, with the narrower part of the panel positioned underneath the wider part.

9 Machine stitch around the edge of the cushion, leaving a ⅝in/1.5cm seam allowance. Trim diagonally across the corners and turn through, making sure that the corners are properly filled out.

TO MAKE THE TASSELS

10 Cut out a piece of thick card 3in/8cm wide. Wrap the crochet thread around the width of the card about 80 times and cut the thread along one edge. Cut a piece of cord 3in/8cm long and tie a knot in it at one end.

11 Open out the bundle of thread and place onto a flat surface, with the cord knot just below the center.

12 Tie a new thread around the bundle of thread and the cord to hold it in place, just above the knot.

13 Pick this basic tassel up by its cord and allow the threads to fall down over the knot. Arrange the threads evenly and wrap the tassel's "neck" with a contrasting piece of thread.

14 Cut a piece of cord 20in/50cm long and wrap each end with a small piece of sticky tape to stiffen them, making them easier to manipulate.

15 Now make the Turk's head knot to complete the tassel. Begin by making a knot to form the base, following the diagrams shown on page 107. Slip the knot over your finger or the end of a pencil, then feed the long end of the cord back through the knot, beginning where the other end emerges. Weave the cord in and out until you have run out of it.

16 Thread the cord of the tassel through the Turk's head and begin to tighten it by pulling one loop and working the cord through the knot. You will need to go around several times until the head of the tassel is the size of a hazelnut.

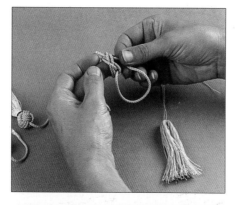

17 Feed the long end of the cord through again until there are three cords side by side over the entire knot. Weave the ends in and trim neatly.

18 Snip the stitching in the corners of the cushion cover and thread the tassel cord through. Stitch securely. Make three other tassels in the same way for the other corners. Insert the cushion pad.

The cushion is edged with elegant tassels.

▶ 31

In any country, the basic furnishings always reflect the materials available to the craftsmen. The design and style of the furniture is dictated, to some extent, by these materials, and in Japan this means the natural plants that grow in the surrounding countryside: reed, cane, and bamboo. Throughout the Far East there is a genuine respect for these raw materials, and the standards of craftsmanship are high. Furniture and artifacts made from these natural materials are extremely collectable, even in Japan itself, and pieces are placed or displayed with great care. Each of the projects in this chapter is potentially collectable, chosen for its style and close attention to detail.

A beautiful, authentic bead and tassel add the finishing touch to an extraordinary lacquered tray. This clever design uses bent rattan cane to support the woven and lacquered paper base, and the cane is positioned to act as a carrying handle too. Like the rattan tray, the floor lamp is inspired by an ancient design made for centuries by local Japanese craftsmen using traditional techniques. The cane and paper lamp is usually made from split bamboo, but on this occasion I chose to use flat band cane because it is more readily available and softer for working with. A tube of paper inserted inside the lamp covers the

light fitting and softens the harsh shadows cast by the unusual dark hexagonal weave. Among the most coveted of all Japanese artifacts is the folding screen. Although it may look like a substantial piece of furniture and therefore difficult to make, this reed screen has been carefully designed so that it can be put together very easily. The simple frame is treated with a rich, dark wood stain that complements the lighter color of the reeds. Finally, like the reed screen, the footstool has an uncluttered, simple shape. It is firm enough to be used as an occasional table or seat, and conforms to the age-old Japanese ideal that furniture should be light, movable, and versatile.

32 ◄

REED & CANE

reed screen

The idealized image of the Japanese way of life is of being able to live in simple, uncluttered rooms with only a few floor cushions and some chests for storage. Although this image is rarely the reality, there is tremendous flexibility in Japanese homes. Where there would be a solid wall in a Western home, there is likely to be a screen in a Japanese home. There are many different types of screen: some, such as *shoji* and *fusama*, are built into the structure, whereas others, such as *tsuitate* and *boyōbu*, are free standing.

Screens can be used to add atmosphere, partition off an area, or provide some privacy. In a multipurpose room, a screen can be used perhaps to create an instant dining area if you have guests, or if you want to hide a work area in the evening.

To make it as simple as possible, this screen has been made from lengths of wood usually used for picture framing. The wood is simply stained and made into three giant "picture frames." The "frames" are then partitioned into panels and fitted with the reed mats.

This type of folding screen is known as a *boyōbu* in Japan. The panels can be filled with paper, bamboo matting, or reeds.

Use the shape of the framing to determine the direction of the reeds:
the flat side for horizontal, the rebated side for vertical. If you can't find ramin framing,
use another hardwood to avoid warping of the frame.

MATERIALS

- Black wood stain
- Dark wood stain—chestnut or yew
- 50ft/15m of 2½in/6cm plain ramin framing
- Miter saw
- Wood glue
- Framing cord and clamp
- Tenon saw or router
- Sanding block
- Clear wax
- Black linen waxed thread
- Pin board and pins
- About 500 30in/76cm reeds
- Scissors
- ⅛ x ¼in/3 x 6mm ramin beading
- 4 2in/5cm brass hinges

Finished size: 48 x 57in/122 x 145cm

1 Mix a little of the black wood stain with some of the dark wood stain in a jar. Try out the resulting mix on a scrap of ramin until the correct color is achieved. Brush the lengths of ramin framing with two coats of the stain.

2 Take the strip of ramin framing and cut a 45-degree miter at one end of it. Measure 56in/142.25cm along the outside edge and cut the second miter to form a long length. Cut six pieces of this length. Next, cut six mitered end pieces 16in/41cm long.

3 Glue the miters and assemble the frames of the screen's three large panels. Hold the corners square with a framing cord and clamp until the glue dries.

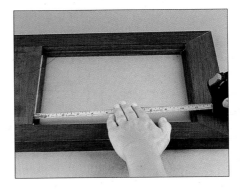

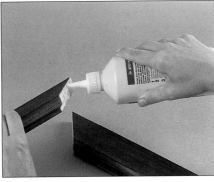

4 Measure the distance between the edges of the recess on the reverse side. Cut nine pieces of wood to this distance, leaving the ends straight, to be used as cross straps. Rout or saw a channel from the front of these cross straps. The channel should be the same width as the frame recess and as deep as the inside edge of the framing. (see picture next column)

5 Arrange the cross straps so that the flat surfaces alternate. Begin with the flat surface facing towards the top on two of the screen panels, and downward on the third. Space the straps 11in/28cm apart and glue into position.

6 Rub the screen down with a fine sanding pad and then apply a coat of clear wax to seal it.

7 Cut two 30in/76cm lengths of linen thread and loop each around two pins spaced 4in/10cm apart on a pinboard. Cut the reeds in half to make lengths of

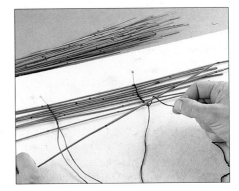

12 Tie and cut off the string from the reed mats.

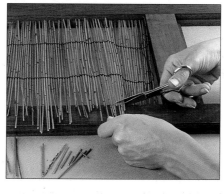

13 Screw brass hinges near the top and bottom of each of the screen's three main panels. The hinges should face in opposite directions between the panels so that they will lie flat against each other when the screen is not in use.

The reeds are finely woven together.

approximately 12in/30cm, and tuck one length between the linen threads. When the reed is in place, cross the threads so that the lower threads are on top, then tuck the next reed in place between the threads.

8 Continue adding reeds until you have a mat about 11in/28cm square. You will need about 75 reeds for each mat. Push the reeds to one side to make a flat edge about 4in/10cm away from the pins.

9 Make eleven more mats in the same way. Lift them, one at a time, onto the reverse side of the screen. Panels that have two flat surfaces on the cross strap should have the reeds running horizontally, whereas the panels that are routed all round should have vertical reeds.

10 Once the mats are in place in the panels, neatly trim the ends of the reeds with scissors to fit.

11 Cut the ramin beading to fit tightly inside the panels, across the cut ends of the reeds. Glue the beading inside the recesses of each panel, checking that the reeds are flat and evenly spaced. (*see picture next column*)

paper and rattan tray

Lacquer work is one of the art styles that the Japanese acquired from the Chinese and have made their own. Wooden trays, bowls, and lunchboxes are traditionally lacquered in either black or deep red, and even the simplest food looks appetizing against the deep shine of the lacquer. Less well known are *tsuzura*, the traditional woven clothes boxes painted with several coats of lacquer.

This lacquered tray is decorated in a similar way, using an unusual, traditional Japanese craft in which strips of paper are folded and woven together to make the mat. This is stabilized with a backing paper, then painted. Kooboo cane, a type of rattan, is used to make the tray handle, completed with a beaded tassel. The tray is surprisingly strong and can be used to serve an assortment of delicacies or pretty crackers.

The beautiful red lacquer bead used in this project has been painted up to 60 times before being carved into the intricate pattern.

▶ 39

JAPAN

Expensive, thick paper is too inflexible for this project. I found that cheaper
construction paper was soft enough to weave together to form the gentle curve of the tray,
but still creased well to make crisply edged strips.

MATERIALS

- *Five sheets white construction paper 16½ x 11¾in (42 x 30cm)*
- *Craft knife*
- *1 small tin Japanese lacquer*
- *Medium-sized paintbrush*
- *Hole punch*
- *2yd/2m length ¼in/6mm kooboo or rattan cane*
- *Strong sewing thread*
- *Drill*
- *1 Chinese lacquer bead*
- *1 small round black wooden bead*
- *1 large round black wooden bead*
- *1 black tassel*

Finished size: 16in/41cm square at base; height 19in/48cm

1 Cut the paper into 1¾in/4.5cm strips. Score each strip along its length with a craft knife, ⅜in/1cm from one edge and ⅝in/1.5cm from the other edge.

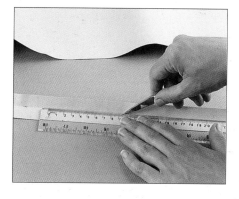

The woven paper base is covered with a high-gloss Japanese lacquer.

2 Fold each strip down the score line, and turn them over so that the largest flap is on top.

3 Weave the strips together to make a panel about 14in/36cm square. Adjust so that the strips are equally spaced and at neat right-angles to each other.

4 Turn the woven mat over. Leaving the corner strips aside, fold over every second strip along the edges of the mat and tuck in under the weave. Tuck in the alternating strips over the weave; this will leave the sides straight.

5 Fold the corner strips over ⅜in/1cm from the side edges and tuck the ends into the weave. Trim off excess paper.

6 Turn over and paint with two coats of lacquer. Punch a hole in each corner, making it the same diameter as the *kooboo* cane.

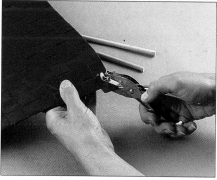

7 Cut two pieces of *kooboo* cane 46in/117cm long and soak in water for about 30 minutes. Bend each piece in half and secure the ends together until dry.

8 Feed the ends of the cane through the holes in the mat. To prevent the paper part of the tray from slipping down the "legs," wrap black thread around the canes about 3in/8cm from the ends and tie off securely.

9 Using a drill set to a slow speed, open out the hole in the Chinese lacquer bead to fit the loop of the tassel. Thread the tassel onto the bead using thread, then add the wooden beads. Tie in place at the point where the canes cross over.

woven cane lamp

Light is an important part of Japanese interiors. Whereas Western homes often have sunlight streaming in at a window, the Japanese prefer the soft, filtered light that comes through *shoji* (a paper and wood screen) or *sudare* (reed and bamboo blinds). At nighttime too, Japanese lights are much warmer. Light is used to create atmosphere, with shadows and interesting textures. Traditional Japanese paper lamps are designed to diffuse light, giving subtle warmth and beauty rather than the bright clarity of a fluorescent or high-wattage bulb.

Paper lamps have been made for centuries in Japan. This particular lamp with its unusual hexagonal weave is traditionally made from split bamboo. As this is not readily available, I have used flat band cane instead. Flat band cane is cut from rattan and is easy to work with, as it requires a minimum amount of soaking to make it pliable. The cane can be left in its natural state or stained with a wood dye. Choose a translucent paper that will allow the light to filter through, but hide the light fitting inside.

The hexagonal weave casts interesting shadows on the table and wall when the lamp is lit.

Flat band and handle cane is easy to stain using a standard wood stain.
You can do this before you begin weaving: make sure you leave enough time for it to dry.
Alternatively, you can simply paint wood stain onto the finished lamp.

MATERIALS

- *17 lengths ½in/12mm flat band cane each 45in/115cm long*
- *13 lengths ½in/12mm flat band cane each 28in/71cm long*
- *8in/20cm diameter lampshade ring*
- *12 spring-loaded clothespins*
- *Scissors*
- *2yd/2m ⁵⁄₁₆in/8mm handle cane*
- *Black wood stain*
- *Wood stain thinner*
- *Hacksaw*
- *1 sheet of Japanese paper 16½ x 11¾in/42 x 30cm*

Finished size: diameter 8in/20cm, height 18in/60cm

1 Dip the canes into water and put into a large plastic bag to keep them damp. Spray them frequently as you work.

2 Bend one of the short lengths of cane around the the lampshade ring. Lift off and use a clothespin to secure the overlap of the two ends of the cane.

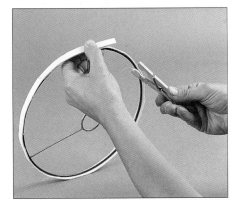

3 Find the center of a long piece of cane and bend it over the cane ring, with the rough side of the cane facing inwards. Open the cane to make a 60-degree angle, and pin into place.

4 Repeat with the other long pieces of cane. As you add the lengths, weave each new piece under the previous one to make a triangle above the cane ring.

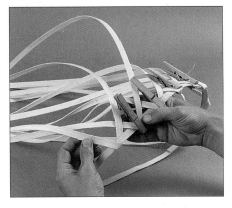

5 Pin each triangle and adjust the spacing so that each of the 13 pieces of cane are the same distance apart. Weave the first and last pieces together to complete the circle.

6 Position the lampshade ring about 1½in/4cm above the cane ring and pin into place. This acts as a guide for the diameter of the lamp and will be moved up as you go to ensure that each horizontal circle of cane is the same size.

7 Take the next short length of cane and fix it with a clothespin, level with the lampshade ring. Weave the length of cane in and out of two of the overlapping uprights to make a triangle.

8 Continue weaving the short length around the lamp's circumference, level with the lampshade ring. Thread the cane under one upright and over the next, and then interlock the two ends above the horizontal ring to produce a series of triangles above the band, and a row of hexagonal spaces below it.

9 Overlap the ends of the cane ring and pin them together. Adjust the overlap until the cane ring fits snugly around the lampshade ring. Move the lampshade ring up 1½in/4cm and pin into place.

10 Continue adding horizontal strips, moving the lampshade ring each time. Check that the sides are straight and the hexagonal shapes are well formed and of even size. When the lamp is approximately 15in/38cm high, unpin the metal ring and dampen the ends of the cane.

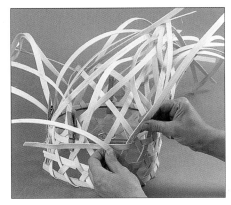

The cane forms an unusual hexagonal weave.

11 To make the folded edge, open out each pair of ends in turn and tuck the front end down to the left in front of its partner. Weave underneath the rows below to secure. Fold the back piece forward and to the right, and tuck under the second row. Trim off all ends neatly with scissors or a craft knife.

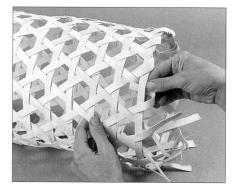

12 Turn the lamp upside down so that the ring you began with is at the top. Secure the lampshade ring on the second row up. Lash the ring by wrapping a long piece of cane around it along its length, and tuck the ends into the weave before trimming.

13 Dampen the handle cane and cut in half. Bend the pieces to make a 8in/20cm-diameter curve in the middle, to fit the diameter of the lamp. Hold the handle in position and use a length of cane to lash around the top edge of the lamp—the row you started with—catching in the handle as you go.

14 Using another length of cane, lash around the lampshade along the base and halfway down its length to hold the handle securely.

15 Measure the length of the "legs" (about 4in/10cm) and saw off the excess cane.

16 Mix a little black wood stain with thinner to make a dark grey stain. Brush the stain over the lamp and leave to dry.

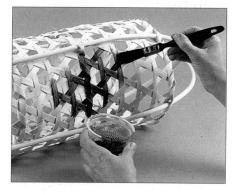

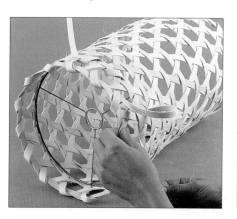

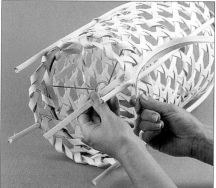

17 Cut the paper in half. Form one half into a loose tube and fit inside the lamp, above the lampshade ring. Turn upside down and fit the other piece of paper in the bottom section of the lamp. Insert a light fitting and a low-energy light bulb.

raffia footstool

Much of the charm of Japanese interiors lies in the low level of the furnishings, where flexibility is the key. Such homes are not only beautiful to look at, but practical too. Because space is at a premium, furniture and rooms in Japanese homes are multipurpose. Rooms used during the day for sitting and eating can be transformed quickly and easily into sleeping areas. Traditional furniture, such as step chests, are useful storage areas but can also provide access to the attic, can be used to display some exquisite ornaments, or even be used as seating.

This footstool is designed with such multiple uses in mind. It is upholstered with a firm crumble foam that is comfortable enough to sit on or to rest your feet but is also solid enough to use as an occasional table. It has a simple loose cover that fits snugly over the square shape.

Use a firm fabric such as rattan or raffia to give a flat, even surface to the footstool so that it can be put to good use as an occasional table.

A local upholsterer made the stylish footstool used as a base for this project to my own specifications. You can adapt the project to any stool: if you can't find one you like in the stores, take this book to a local craftsperson and ask them to make one in a similar shape.

BASIC SEWING SKILLS REQUIRED

MATERIALS
- *36 x 12in/90 x 30cm footstool*
- *Masking tape*
- *Black wood stain*
- *Clear wax*
- *1yd/1m of 55in-/140cm-wide raffia fabric*
- *Sewing kit and sewing machine*

Finished size: 36 x 12 x 10in/ 90 x 30 x 25cm

1 Brush black wood stain onto the footstool's legs. Leave to dry.

2 Apply a coat of clear wax to the legs. Lift the stool onto a table and cover with the fabric; it should reach down to the tabletop all around. Trim off any excess.

3 With the reverse side of the fabric facing out, crease the first corner and pin down the length of the edge of the footstool. (*see picture top of next column*)

4 Pin the other three corners to match. Run your finger along the grain of the fabric to make sure it lies centrally and neatly on the stool. Adjust if necessary.

5 Lift the cover off and lay the first corner on a flat surface. Check that the pins are following the same thread of the weave all the way down both sides of the seam on each corner.

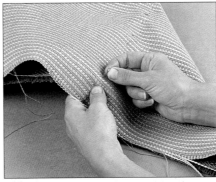

6 Machine stitch the seams, reinforcing the top by reverse stitching. Machine stitch with a triple zigzag stitch down each seam. Trim close to the stitching.

7 Fit the cover onto the footstool. Turn up the bottom hem so that it is about ⅜in/1cm below the bottom of the stool.

8 Remove the cover from the stool, trim the hem to 2–3in/5–8cm, and zigzag stitch along the edge. Turn the seams at each end of the footstool to face each other. Cross the seams along the bottom edge of the hem and pin in opposite directions to reduce bulk.

9 Check that the hem follows the straight grain all the way round. Then machine stitch from the right side, ¾in/2cm from the fold.

10 Fit the cover back onto the footstool.

The raffia fabric used in the footstool is both beautifully textured and very hardwearing.

JAPAN

REED & CANE

paper

▶ 51

P aper is a fundamental ingredient in creating the atmosphere and character of Japanese style. To Western eyes, paper is a cheap, throwaway commodity, but in Japan its inherent qualities are exploited to the full. There are many different Japanese papers, some handmade, and others, such as *chugata*, printed with bright patterns to look almost like fabric. The most common paper in Japan is *washi* paper. This white paper is used to make everything from lights to blinds and screens. I used a similar looking paper as the basis for a stunning paper hanging. Pieces of a different, lacy Japanese paper were sandwiched between layers of abaca tissue to create a translu-

cent pattern that looks equally good hung against the wall or in front of a window. Light, whether it comes from sunlight or a lamp, is much softer and warmer when it filters through paper. I chose an unusual crumpled paper called *momigami* to make a tall cane and paper lamp. The lamp holds three tea light candles, one at each "bump" in its elegant curved shape. The open archways, which allow easy access to the tea lights, can either be used as a decorative feature or, if you want your lamp to look simpler, hidden away on the reverse side. On a summer's evening, this lightweight lamp can be hung outside.

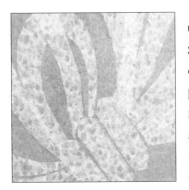

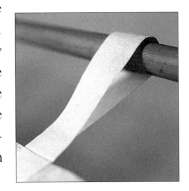

Despite its delicate appearance, paper can be used to make some quite substantial containers. Simple papier-mâché is transformed into a highly decorative technique by using beautiful Japanese paper rather than newsprint. I chose a delicate mulberry paper in two contrasting colors to make some classic Japanese bowls, and used a selection of papers to turn a simple vase made from cut bamboo into something quite special.

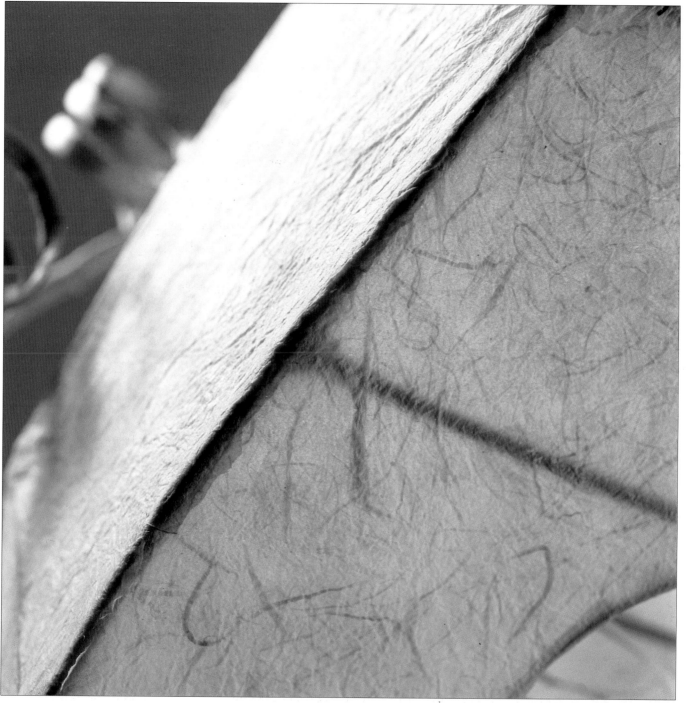

PAPER

paneled
paper hanging

The concept of *oku* (distance) is one of the most important aspects of Japanese architecture. Optical illusions are often used to make rooms appear larger, or gardens longer, than they really are. The Japanese use translucent paper to create a feeling of space and dimension because it leads the eye through and beyond the surface. *Washi* blinds and *shoji* (checkerboard screens) both use this concept to great effect, and this stunning paper hanging was inspired by both.

The Japanese love to suggest the impression of movement by cropping an image, leaving the viewer to imagine the rest. This striking design was built up using a delicate handmade Japanese paper sandwiched between squares of translucent tissue paper. The design is based on the traditional Japanese talisman known as *noshi*, which is an abbreviation of *noshiawaba*, which means "flattened-out abalone." In the past, strips of abalone, a type of shellfish, were tied together to make a gift to the gods. Nowadays *noshi* are tied with pretty pieces of paper and attached to gifts at New Year as an emblem of good fortune.

▶ 55

Hang this dynamic paper hanging against a plain wall or as a flat blind over a window so that the light can filter through the layers of paper.

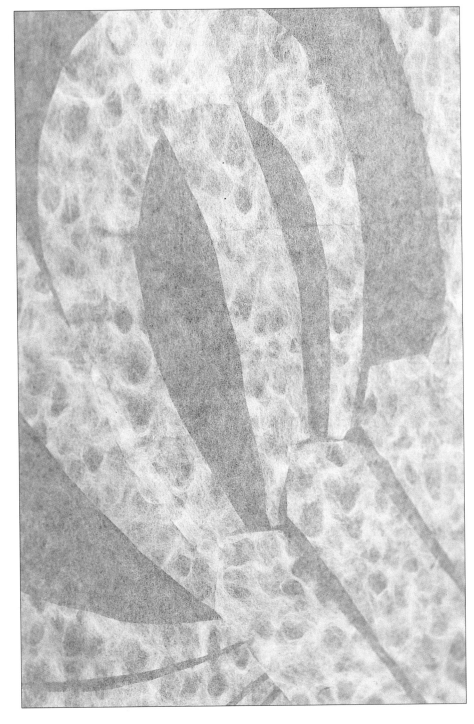

The delicate Japanese paper used in this project is made by dropping water onto the fibers to create the characteristic holes. If you can't find this paper in your craft store, you can use any hand-made Japanese paper. Try using different papers for different effects.

MATERIALS

◆ *1 roll graph paper*
◆ *Scissors*
◆ *Pencil and ruler*
◆ *10 sheets of LX or Lens paper (Tissuetex)*
◆ *Spray mount*
◆ *Japanese paper with holes*
◆ *Iron*
◆ *Fusible bonding web*

Finished size: 40in/102cm square (excluding hanging tabs)

1 If you want to make the hanging as a window blind, measure the window where you wish to hang it, taking into account whether you want the blind to hang inside or outside the window's recess. Cut the piece of graph paper to this exact size.

2 Mark out nine squares on the graph paper and then turn to the template on page 109. Using a pencil, carefully copy the template onto the graph paper, square by square, to create an enlarged version of the design.

The delicate paper and the pale colors used in the hanging contrast beautifully with the bold, sweeping lines of the design.

3 Trace the shapes onto the Japanese paper with intermittent soft pencil lines. Cut the design out, just inside the lines.

4 Cut out nine squares of LX/Lens paper (Tissuetex) to the same size as the ones drawn on the graph paper, and position on top of it. Spray the reverse side of the Japanese paper pieces and stick onto the LX/Lens paper (Tissuetex) squares.

5 Make the main hanging from nine squares of LX/Lens paper (Tissuetex), stuck together with fusible bonding web. Allow a 2in/5cm hem allowance all around the corner pieces, and add ¼in/6mm to the edges that will be joined to allow for a ½in/12mm overlap.

6 Cut out the outside middle sections from the LX/Lens paper (Tissuetex) with a 2in/5cm hem allowance on the outside, and add ¼in/6mm overlap allowance to the other edges.

7 Finally, cut out the center square with a ¼in/6mm overlap allowance all round.

8 Mark and cut ⅜in-/1cm-long strips of fusible bonding web. Work in rows across the hanging. Iron a strip of bonding web to the edges of the LX/Lens paper (Tissuetex). Peel off the backing paper and iron the next panel in position, overlapping the paper by a margin of about ½in/12mm.

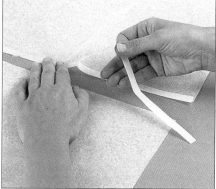

9 Continue putting together the three rows of the hanging, and then join them as in Step 8.

10 Lay the hanging face down on the graph paper and line up the seams between the marked lines. Spray the decorated squares, and stick them face down onto the framework of the hanging. (You will need to reverse the layout so that the squares are in the correct position when the hanging is turned over to the right side.)

11 Fold over the hem allowance on the edge of the hanging and open out. Cut 2in/5cm lengths of Japanese paper and stick along the edges of the hanging, between the corner squares. Spray the hem and fold it over, cutting away the corners to reduce bulk.

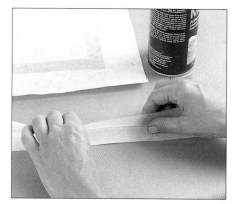

12 Cut out fourteen 3 x 10in/8 x 25cm pieces of LX/Lens paper (Tissuetex) and spray on one side with glue. Fold the paper in three, mask the strips, and spray the last 2in/5cm of each end.

▶ 57

13 Fix the tabs, equally spaced, along the top and bottom edges of the hanging. Hang using a thin pole of bamboo threaded through each row of tabs.

tall vases

One of the most delightful crafts in Japan is the art of gift-wrapping. Beautiful boxes and packets, created from precisely folded card or paper, are tied and finished with exquisite gift tags. Such packages were the inspiration for these unusual paper vases. The simple bamboo container is wrapped as if it were a gift and then tied with a decorative label and raffia.

The bamboo is cut just below the joint to make a vase and then covered with corrugated paper to produce an unusual ribbed surface. Soften the rough surface with a layer of tissue paper papier-mâché, and complete the package with a pretty label based on the traditional Japanese gift tag. *Chiyogami* is Japanese paper patterned with brightly-colored designs. It is available in small packs for *origami*. Choose colors that complement the flowers you intend to put in the vase, or the décor of your home. Complete the label with handmade paper and a design painted using black ink and a traditional bamboo brush. Copy symbols from some Japanese text, or simply use your imagination to create a Japanese-style motif.

The bamboo container under the paper wrapping makes the vases waterproof and adds weight so that they can be used to display a variety of plant material.

58 ◀

Corrugated paper is similar to card except that one side is smooth
and the other fluted. It is used as a packaging material, especially for framed pictures,
and can be bought by the roll in stationery shops.

MATERIALS

- ◆ *1 bamboo pole*
- ◆ *12in/30cm square corrugated paper*
- ◆ *Scissors*
- ◆ *Double-sided sticky tape*
- ◆ *White craft glue*
- ◆ *1 packet white tissue paper*
- ◆ *Small sponge*
- ◆ *1 sheet plain Japanese* origami *paper*
- ◆ *1 sheet patterned Japanese* origami *paper*
- ◆ *1 sheet white* shoji *paper or other handmade paper*
- ◆ *Medium Japanese paintbrush*
- ◆ *Black ink*
- ◆ *Natural raffia*

Finished size: 9½ x 3in/24 x 8cm

1 Cut a length of bamboo just below one of its joints (where the bamboo "bulges") to make the solid base of the vase, and then make another cut 10in/25cm higher to form its height.

2 Measure and cut a strip of corrugated paper to the same height as you have chosen for the vase, so that the grooves ("flutes") run horizontally around it.

3 Wrap the corrugated paper around the length of bamboo. Crease and mark with a pencil the point where the paper overlaps, and cut along the line.

4 Stick the corrugated paper snugly around the vase with a length of double-sided sticky tape at the overlap. (*see picture next column*)

5 Dilute the white craft glue with five parts water. Tear the tissue paper into long, thin, irregular pieces and paste onto the vase. Work the paper into the flutes with the sponge.

6 Allow the vase to dry overnight away from direct heat.

7 Cut rectangles of plain and patterned Japanese paper to make a label for the front of the vase.

8 Cut a piece of *shoji* paper to fit onto the label. Use the Japanese brush and ink to draw motifs to resemble Japanese script.

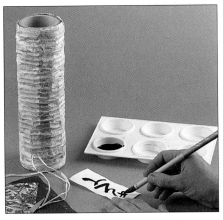

9 Tie the label in position on the front of the vase with natural raffia.

10 The vase is now ready to use. As it is cut from just below a bamboo joint, it is able to hold water, so it is perfect for an arrangement of fresh flowers.

JAPAN

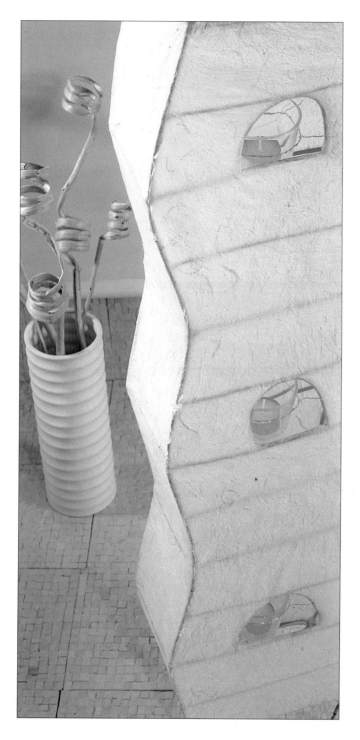

momigami lamp

Paper lamps are designed not to give a bright light, but rather to create a soft, warm atmosphere in a room. The Japanese prefer the interesting effect of shadows cast from a diffused light, and believe that subtle light and shade enhances interiors. The ubiquitous round white *Akari* lamp (shown on page 50), first created in the 1950s by Isamu Noguchi, is still the choice for many first-time homemakers, and is found in both traditional and modern interiors. The simple combination of paper and thin strips of bamboo inspired this lamp.

Instead of bamboo, the framework of the lamp is made from penambang cane. This is a thin, very pliable cane that can be bent into shape while dry. It is sold by weight, and comes in very long lengths that vary slightly in thickness. Choose thin pliable lengths for the curved sides, and thicker, straight pieces for the cross struts. The lamp can be wired with miniature halogen lights, or fitted with tea lights as shown. Whichever you choose, it should be treated with a fire-retardant spray and care should always be taken to prevent the lamp from being knocked over.

▶ 61

The little archways give easy access to tea lights. For greater stability the lamp can be hung from the cross struts at the top.

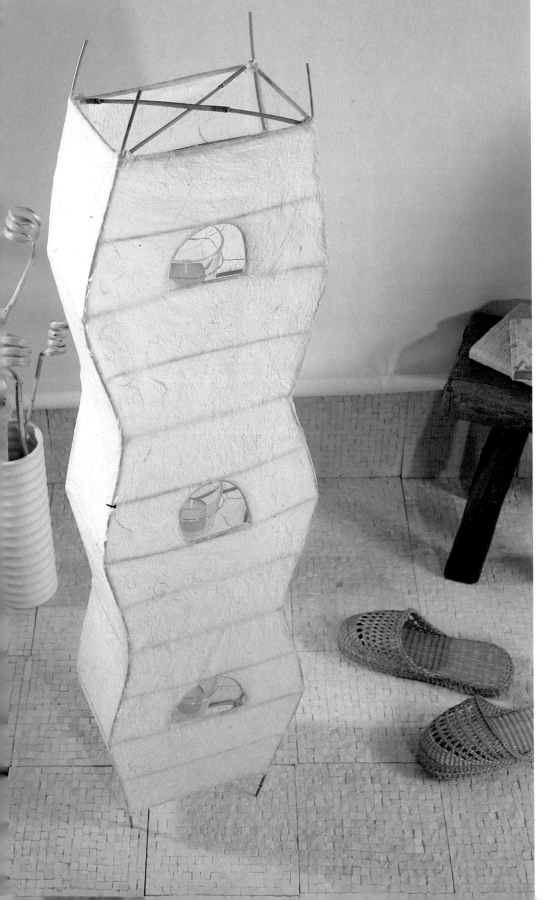

It is essential to be accurate when measuring and taping the cross struts on this delicate lamp, to make sure its framework is perfectly symmetrical and straight. It will help to mark two lines 2¾in/7cm apart on the work surface as a guide.

MATERIALS

- ◆ 16oz/454g ¼in/6mm penambang cane
- ◆ Double-sided sticky tape ¼in/6mm wide
- ◆ Lightweight masking tape
- ◆ 3yd/3m 24-gauge silver-plated wire
- ◆ Wire cutters
- ◆ 3 tea lights with glass holders
- ◆ Natural-colored momigami paper
- ◆ White craft glue
- ◆ Fire-retardant spray

Finished size: 5 x 10 x 40in/ 13 x 25 x 102cm

1 Cut four 48in/120cm lengths of the thinnest, most pliable cane for the curved edges of the lamp. Cut the graded cross struts from straight, strong sections. You will need six 10in/25.5cm long pieces, twelve 8½in/22cm pieces, and eight 7½in/18.5cm pieces.

2 Begin with a short cross strut and position it 2in/5cm from the end of one of the long lengths of cane. Use double-sided sticky tape to secure it in the first instance, and then cover the join with a thin strip of masking tape.

The tea lights are placed in decorative arches along the length of the lamp.

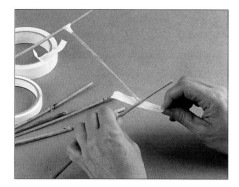

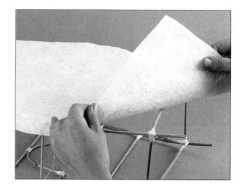

5 Cut fourteen 4¾ in/12cm side struts. Tape these to every second cross strut using thin strips of masking tape. Then trim the "legs" at each end of the lamp with scissors.

6 Cut and fit single diagonal struts inside the lamp to strengthen the structure. Fit crossed diagonal struts at the top to allow you to hang it up.

7 Make a coil of wire to fit around a glass tea light holder. Wrap wire around the length of the coil to strengthen it. Attach the ring in the center of the lamp's frame behind one of the archways with a length of wire to each corner. Do this for each of the three tea lights.

3 Join the other end to another of the long pieces of cane in the same way. Tape the next size of cross strut about 2¾in/7cm further down the lamp. Continue adding the cross struts in order: short, medium, long, medium, short, and so on, until the three "bumps" of the lamp have been created.

4 Make the back of the lamp to match. Cut three pieces of thin, pliable cane to make portholes for the nightlights—tape the center of the cane to the center of the longest cross struts, then bend the ends to make an arch and tape to the next cross strut.

9 Turn the frame over and stick a similar piece of *momigami* paper to the reverse side in the same way. Once the paper has dried, cut around the inside of the archways, leaving a ¼in/6mm seam allowance. Glue the cut edges inside the frames of the archways.

10 Tear or cut the excess paper down the sides of the framework. Cut the top and bottom edges with a ¼in/6mm seam allowance and glue neatly inside.

11 Stand the framework on its side and apply paper to the sides of the lamp in the same way. Allow the paper to dry before moving the lamp.

12 Tear or cut off the excess paper and paste down any ragged edges to complete the lamp. Spray the lamp inside and out with a fire-retardant spray.

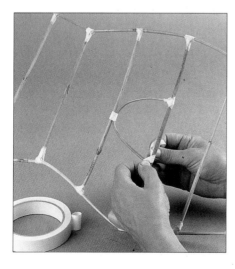

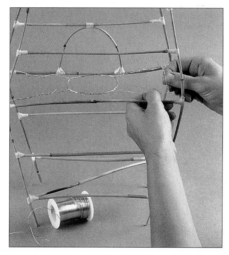

8 Cut out a piece of *momigami* paper slightly larger than the front of the framework. Dilute the white craft glue with five parts water. Use a brush or sponge to apply the glue to one side of the paper. Lay the pasted paper over the framework and press down gently along the edges. Allow the paper to dry. (*see picture next column*)

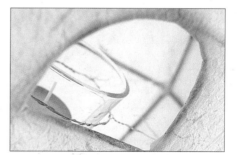

papier-mâché bowls

Japan has always been a nation of craftsmen working with a variety of natural materials such as wood, bamboo, cane, and of course paper. Japanese craftspeople believe that such natural materials infuse warmth and beauty into otherwise inanimate objects. There are two quite different schools of craft in Japan—the exquisitely fine furniture and artifacts of the Imperial Court, and the more utilitarian folk arts. These papier-mâché bowls come from the folk art tradition of making things to be used rather than as decorative objects. Their straightforward simplicity gives them a universal appeal.

Japan is famous for its beautiful handmade paper, which is now available all over the world. You can use almost any type of paper to make papier-mâché, but a thinner paper gives a much smoother finish to the bowls. I used a fine mulberry paper with a silky surface. Two contrasting shades like the deep red and off-white used here are typical of the Japanese style. You only need a couple of layers of the deep red, and then continue building up the layers in off-white until the darker color is completely covered.

▶ 65

These bowls have any number of possible uses. Before using for rice or noodles, spray the inside with a matt varnish. Wipe with a damp cloth to clean.

Most styles of bowl can be used for this project, as long as the shape is wider at the top than at the bottom so that the finished papier-mâché can be lifted out. If the bowl you use as a mold is plastic, you will not need to line it with aluminum foil.

MATERIALS
◆ *Large shallow bowl to use as mold*
◆ *Vaseline*
◆ *Aluminum foil*
◆ *White craft glue*
◆ *1 large sheet handmade rhododendron paper*
◆ *Small sponge*
◆ *1 large sheet handmade natural-colored mulberry paper*

1 Smear the inside of the bowl with a thin layer of Vaseline. If the bowl is ceramic, like the one we used here, cover with aluminum foil, smoothing the foil until it is as flat as possible.

4 Keep adding the paper until the entire bowl is covered with a couple of layers. Leave the top edge fairly ragged.

7 Once the papier-mâché is complete and dry, lift it out of the bowl and peel off the aluminum foil.

2 Dilute the white craft glue with five parts water. The next stage is to roughly tear up the colored rhododendron paper into 2–4in/5–10cm pieces.

3 Using a sponge, cover the paper with the diluted glue and paste the pieces on top of the foil, or directly onto the bowl if it is plastic. (*see picture next column*)

5 Allow the papier-mâché to dry overnight, away from direct heat.

6 Cover the colored papier-mâché with several layers of natural-colored mulberry paper. You may need to repeat the process several times until the dye stops seeping through the natural paper. (*see picture next column*)

8 Cover the outside of the bowl with another layer of rhododendron paper and allow to dry balanced upside down on a jug.

The edges of the bowls are deliberately left rough and untrimmed for a delicate feathered effect, which shows off the two contrasting colors of paper.

PAPER

wood & stone

▶ 69

Natural materials are an essential characteristic of the Japanese home and its surroundings. Indeed, the use of wood and stone stems from the desire to replicate the peace and tranquillity of the outdoors inside, with plants and natural materials enhancing the otherwise austere surroundings. Japanese gardens are traditionally very much a part of the interior of the home. Most can be enjoyed from indoors by drawing back a screen or blind. If, however, you have no room for a garden, make a miniature version indoors. Hide a plastic pond liner inside a beautiful wooden box and enjoy the relaxing sound of water bubbling over the stones. If you want to keep the

water garden on the patio, you will need to use a water-resistant wood such as cedar. This same wood has been used to make an unusual circular bath mat that immediately evokes an oriental look. Complete the effect with the ubiquitous white kimono-style bathrobe.

Carefully chosen accessories do play a vital part in creating Japanese style. The Japanese home is often a strange mix of the modern and the traditional, where simple minimalist furnishings contrast with ornate accessories that reflect the expert craftsmanship of the past. Lacquer-ware is one of the most instantly recognizable of these ancient crafts.

The high-gloss finish in black or red is synonymous with Japan, and a simple tray becomes a work of art when decorated with a mass of swirling golden waves. Waves are also the decorative theme for the stone candle holder. The concentric semi-circular pattern is a traditional *komon* or "small pattern," known as "blue waves." Use the candle holder in the house or on the patio on a summer evening.

WOOD & STONE

water garden

The Japanese believe that plants and other natural forms encourage animistic spirits to remain in and around the house to preserve the prosperity and happiness of the inhabitants. Their gardens have three main elements: plants, stones, and water. The gardens often have manmade objects amidst the lush foliage to symbolize the links between man and his environment, and are carefully planned to create visual interest. Gardens are designed for viewing from inside the house or from a particular spot on the veranda. The plants are arranged carefully so that large-leafed plants are in the foreground and smaller-leafed shrubs further away, to give the impression of distance.

Each garden has a focal point, often a small bridge, a bamboo fountain, or an *objet d'art*. The focus of this miniature garden is the water bubbling from the large drilled pebble in the center of the stones. The pebble pool liner has a trough on two sides for indoor plants. If you want to make the water garden for the patio, use cedar wood for the box and fill the trough with outdoor plants.

Walnut hardwood has a deep gray-brown color that complements the color of the pebbles. Elm, oak, or ash can also be used, depending on the color of your furnishings.

The water garden has been designed so that the legs at the corners bear the weight of the water-filled pool liner. As a result the box can simply be glued together, avoiding difficult joints and screws.

MATERIALS

- *3yd/3m planks 6½in/160mm wide of ½in/12mm walnut hardwood*
- *Tenon saw or router*
- *Sanding block*
- *1yd/1m 2in/50mm square-section walnut hardwood*
- *Wood glue*
- *3yd/3m 1in/25mm square-section pine*
- *G-clamps*
- *Clear wax*
- *29in/74cm square pebble pool liner*
- *Water pump*
- *Assorted large pebbles*
- *Large drilled pebble*
- *Pot plants*

Finished size: 30in/76cm square

1 Cut two pieces of ½in/12mm walnut 30in/76cm, and two 30½in/77cm. Rout a ¼in/6mm channel across each end of the longer planks. Then rub down the rough edges with the sanding block.

2 Cut the square-section walnut into 9in/22.5cm lengths and sand the edges.

3 Mark a line 1½in/4cm down from the top edge of the planks. Glue the legs at each end of the shorter planks and place a weight on top until dry.

4 Measure and cut the pine to fit between the legs and then glue into place, level with the tops of the legs.

5 Assemble the box by gluing the joints and remaining sides of the legs. Clamp the pieces together until dry. Cut and glue a strap of pine to the remaining sides to complete the box.

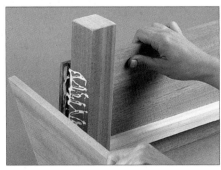

6 Rub down any rough edges on the box, and apply two coats of clear wax.

7 Position the box where it is to stand and insert the pebble pool liner. Fit the pump into the basin and cover with water. Fit the lid over the pump.

8 Arrange a few pebbles around the pump hole and then fit the drilled pebble on top. Adjust the height of the drilled pebble until the pump tube is just below the top of the drilled hole.

9 Switch on the pump to check that the water is bubbling out evenly. Alter the height and angle of the drilled pebble if required, until the water is flowing evenly over the stone.

10 Fill the flat area with the remaining pebbles. Use small pebbles to hide any plastic that is showing around the edge of the box.

11 Fill up the trough with plants. Use a variety of heights and colors to make the display as attractive as possible.

The sound of water playing gently onto stones has a calming effect.

WOOD & STONE

bath mat

The moon-viewing windows found in many Japanese houses inspired the circular shape of this bath mat. The Japanese are moon-lovers rather than sun-worshipers and have moon-viewing parties in just the same way as we in the West might have friends over to enjoy a barbecue on a summer's day. Their houses often have circular windows with interlaced bamboo latticework set into a wall facing the full moon.

Wood is an essential part of the Japanese art of bathing. The deep wooden baths are usually made from the much-prized Kyoto *hinoki* (Japanese cypress). This wood produces a wonderful, heady fragrance as the steam from the hot water rises through the slatted lids. I have used Western red cedar because it is more readily available and can be cut to size by your local lumberyard. Cedarwood has an attractive smell and, because it is not affected by water, requires no treatment other than a rub down with some sandpaper. In the course of time the color will fade to an attractive soft gray-brown.

The wood slats are held together with natural sisal rope. A loop has been left at one side to allow the mat to be hung up to dry.

It is much easier to make accurate straight holes through the wooden slats if you use a tower drill. This is a drill on a stand that is lowered with a lever at exactly 90 degrees.

MATERIALS
- *10yd/10m 1in/25mm square Western red cedar*
- *Pencil and T-square*
- *Strong thread*
- *Tape measure*
- *Fret- or bandsaw*
- *Sanding block*
- *Fine sanding pad*
- *7/16in/11mm drill bit and drill*
- *2yd/2m 3/8in/1cm sisal rope*
- *Sticky tape*
- *26 veneer pins*
- *Hammer*

Finished size: diameter 25in/63.5cm

1 Cut out ten pieces of cedar wood 24in/61cm long and three pieces 25in/64cm long. Arrange these slats on a flat surface to form a circular shape, with the longer lengths in the middle. Use a T-square to mark a line along the center of the circle, across all the slats, to serve as a guide to make sure that the slats are lined up.

2 Cut twenty-four 1in/2.5cm blocks of cedar and intersperse them between the thirteen wooden slats, about 8in/20cm apart, to act as temporary spacers. Before proceeding check that the center lines of all the slats are still aligned.

3 Tie a pencil to one end of a long length of strong thread. Hold the other end of the thread firmly in the center of the middle slat and carefully draw a circle across all the thirteen slats, keeping the tension tight to keep it accurate. Extend the circle to the farthest edge of the wood, making it as large as it can possibly go.

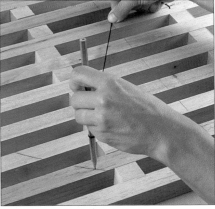

The handsome cedar wood used in this project will mellow with age and use, and it will become a cherished bathroom accessory.

78 ◀

4 Check that the diameter of the resulting circle measures the same lengthways as widthways, then carefully cut along the marked lines using a fret- or bandsaw. Rub down any rough edges, and then smooth down with the fine sanding pad to make the mat "bare feet friendly."

5 With a pencil, mark the positions of the rope holes onto each of the slats—about 1¼in/3cm either side of the center line you marked earlier. The safe and effective way to do this is to place the first slat sideways onto a piece of scrap wood and firmly drill the two holes right through into the wood below. Drill the other slats using the same method.

6 Rub down any raw edges and then arrange the slats in order, upside down. Drill a small pilot hole above the rope holes of each slat to allow the veneer pin heads to be hidden.

7 Tape up the ends of the ropes with sticky tape so that they are rigid enough to be fed through the holes. Beginning in the middle of the rope, feed one end through each row of holes.

8 Reinsert the wooden spacers between the slats and pull the rope tight, leaving a small loop at the top to act as a handle. Hammer the veneer pins into each hole and through the rope to secure it, then sink their heads into the wood with a steel punch. Remove the temporary spacers. (*see picture next column*)

9 Tie the rope in a knot at each end and then cut off the excess. Sand off any pencil marks and turn the mat over to the correct side.

The mat is secured with attractive knots.

tea tray

The theatricality of the Japanese tea ceremony, known as *Cha-no-yu*, is as popular today as it was in ancient times, and even some of the most modern homes have a tea ceremony room. There are strict rules governing the cleaning and setting out of utensils, the warming of the tea bowls, and the preparing and serving of the tea. There are no corners cut when entertaining the honored guest (*Okyakusama*) and everything must be just perfect.

This beautiful lacquered tea tray adds a touch of luxury to even the simplest fare. The tray has been constructed very simply from pre-cut sections of wood, then primed and painted with several coats of Japanese lacquer, an extremely high-gloss paint. Traditionally the gold is applied as gold leaf, but I have used an italic gold pen to achieve a similar effect. The swirling waves are a recurring theme in Japanese design and are often used in *tsutsugaki*, a paste-resist dyeing technique. The gold lines must be drawn with fluid natural movements to achieve flowing lines and soft curves. Mistakes can be washed off the lacquer if you use water-based gold ink.

Dark colors appeal to the Japanese and the luster of the black lacquer contrasts beautifully with the gold design.

JAPAN

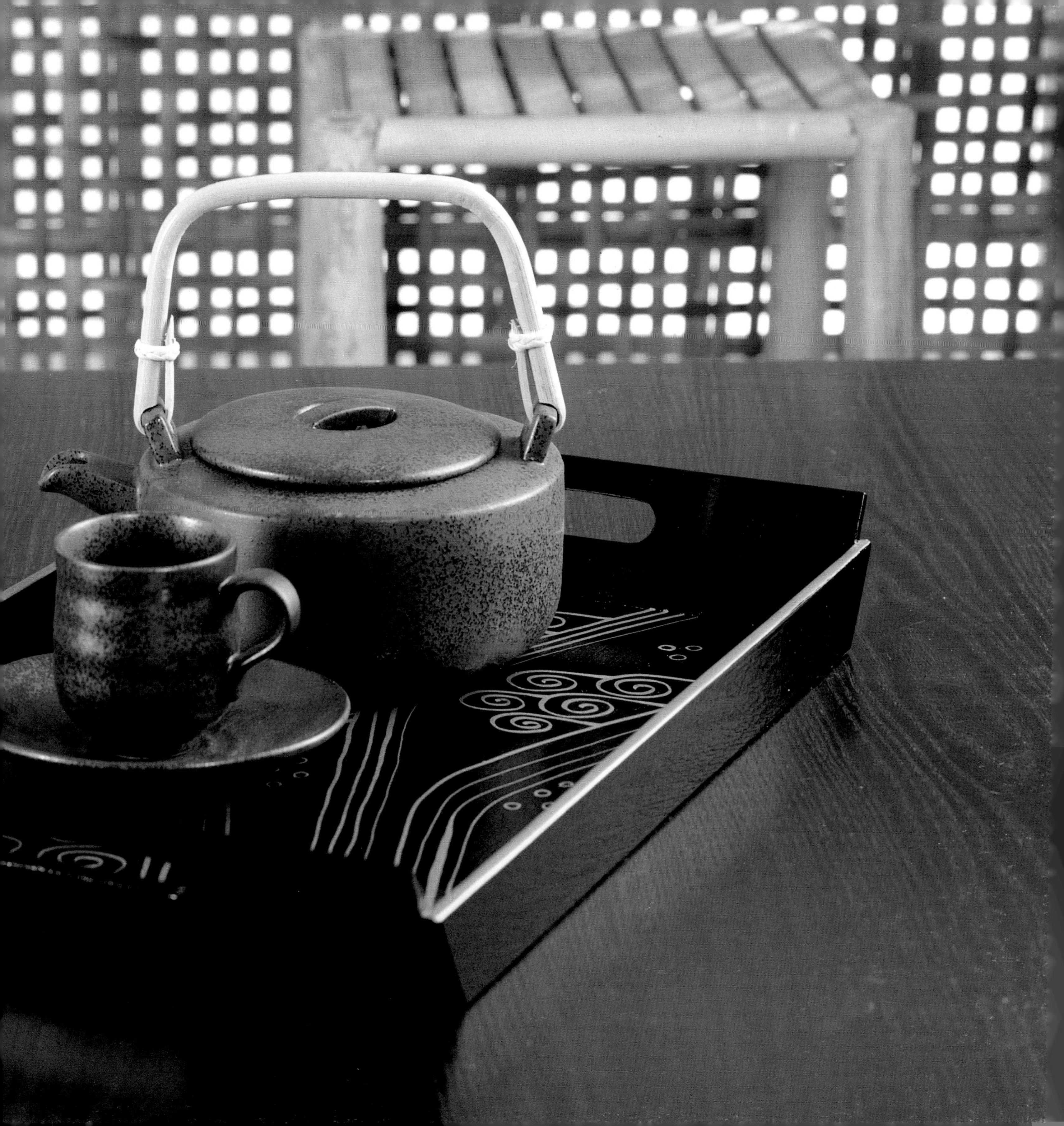

Before painting the tray with the lacquer paint, wipe it with a damp cloth to
remove any dust, and make sure you apply the paint in a clean, dust-free environment
as the high-gloss paint will emphasize any dirt or imperfections.

BASIC WOODWORKING SKILLS
AND KNOWLEDGE OF POWER TOOLS
REQUIRED

MATERIALS

- *20in/500mm square ¼in/6mm MDF*
- *Pencil and ruler*
- *¾in/20mm hole drill bit and drill*
- *Jigsaw or fretsaw*
- *Sanding block*
- *Miter saw*
- *Wood glue*
- *Masking tape*

- ◆ *Wood filler*
- ◆ *Undercoat*
- ◆ *Black Japanese lacquer*
- ◆ *Chalk or chinagraph pencil*
- ◆ *Gold italic nib fiber-tipped pen*
- ◆ *Spray varnish*

Finished size (at widest point):
12¼ x 18¾ x 2½in/31 x 48 x 6cm

The tray is decorated with a modern, stylized version of an old Japanese wave pattern.

1 Cut out the following pieces from MDF:
base: 11⅞ x 16in/30 x 41cm
two long sides: 1½ x 18in/4 x 46cm
two handles: 2¾ x 11⅞in/7 x 30cm.

2 Mark a line 4in/10cm in from each end of the two handle pieces, and measure down 1in/2.5cm to find the position of the handle holes.

3 Drill two large holes at either end of these markings. Mark their centers first, then secure the handle pieces with a clamp over a piece of scrap wood and drill the ¾in/20mm holes right through to the wood below (the safe way.)

4 Draw lines between the holes along the top and bottom: these mark out the oblong shapes with rounded ends which will be cut out for the tray's handles.

5 Form the handles by cutting along the lines with the jig- or fretsaw. Sand off any rough edges.

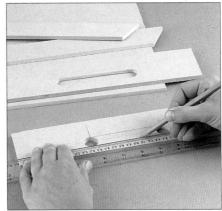

6 To miter the ends of the sides, set the miter saw at a 60-degree angle. Cut across one end and then mark out exactly where you want the other miter to begin. Cut the 60-degree angle from that mark. Cut the other side to match.

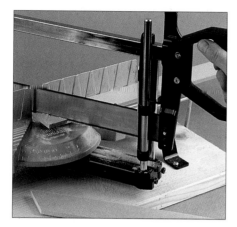

7 Sand the bottom edge of the handle pieces to make a precise 60-degree angle. Make a matching angle on the short sides of the base.

8 Carefully glue the pieces of the tray together, using masking tape to hold the edges flush as the glue dries. Allow the tray to dry overnight.

9 Fill any gaps in the seams with wood filler and then sand down all the edges to form soft curves.

10 Paint the entire tray with undercoat and leave to dry overnight.

11 After making sure that the tray is thoroughly dry, rub it down, top and bottom, with a sanding pad.

12 Wipe the tray with a damp cloth to remove any dust, and paint with two coats of black Japanese lacquer. Make sure you do this in an area away from drafts, as the high-gloss surface of the lacquer makes it all too easy to see any bits of dust and dirt that have been accidentally picked up.

13 Enlarge the tray design on page 110 between the vertical lines, using a photocopier, to the size of the base of the tray (11⅞ x 16in/30 x 41cm).

14 On the enlarged photocopy, use a thick darning needle to make lines of tiny pinpricks close together along the lines of the design.

15 Rub the reverse side of the photocopy thoroughly with a sanding pad to remove the bumps caused by the pinpricks, and position the piece of paper inside the tray.

16 Rub the chalk or chinagraph pencil over each of the holes to transfer the design onto the tray.

17 Lift the paper and carefully join the dots with the chalk or chinagraph pencil, using the original pattern on page 110 as your reference.

18 Draw over the chalk lines with the gold pen. To achieve an authentic, calligraphic effect, relax your arm and try to draw freely, with long flowing movements, so that the lines are soft and natural rather than juddery and stilted.

19 Color in the top edge of the sides of the tray with the gold pen. Spray the finished design with a gloss varnish.

20 The tray is now ready to use. When you need to clean it, avoid using strong detergents or abrasive cleaners; simply wipe with a damp cloth dipped in warm soapy water and pat dry.

▶ 8 3

candle holder

Design is an essential element in Japanese culture, and similar patterns and motifs recur in all types of craft, from ceramics and utensils to clothes and *objets d'art*. The distinctive *Seigaiha* or "blue wave" pattern used on the sides of this concrete candle holder is one of the small patterns, known as *Komon*, that have been used in Japan for centuries. These unique patterns were first designed for the clothes of the Samurai at the beginning of the 17th century. They are typically Japanese and were not inspired by foreign imports. In the beginning many of the patterns were restricted to the ruling classes (*Daimyo*), but by the mid-19th century, people from all walks of life were using *Edo Komon Kire* (cloth with small patterns).

Concrete is not a material that can be used for fine detail. It can be made from various proportions of cement, sand, and gravel, depending on the intended use. I used a mixture of sharp sand and cement to produce a finely grained rough texture, and created the relief pattern on the inside of a simple wooden mold using lengths of string.

The Japanese are great collectors of interesting objects. This concrete candle holder makes an interesting focal point in the home, patio, or garden.

Hardware and home improvement stores supply readymade concrete mixes, but these are not usually suitable as even the bags containing so-called "fine" cement often contain quite large stones. To make perfect cement, it is always better to purchase the cement and sand separately.

MATERIALS

- *1yd/1m 4¾in/12cm tongue-and-groove pine*
- *Heavy-duty craft knife*
- *8in/20cm square MDF*
- *Drill and drill bits*
- *Tracing paper and pencil*
- *Thick string*
- *Pins*
- *Wood glue*
- *Fine nails*
- *Clear plastic wrap*
- *Cement*
- *Sharp sand*
- *Four plastic cups*
- *Four small candles*

Finished size: 8¼in/21cm square

1 Cut two 8¼in/21cm and two 8in/20cm lengths of tongue-and-groove pine. Using a heavy-duty craft knife or a small saw, carefully cut one side of the groove off the edge of the lengths of pine to leave a channel for the MDF to fit snugly into.

String is used to create the striking pattern of undulating waves on the sides of the candle holder.

2 Mark a ½in/12mm border on each side of the longer lengths of pine and drill two pilot holes for the nails. This area should be kept clear of the design.

3 Trace the design on page 110 and position on the pine. Use a pin to transfer the design to the wood. Stick pieces of string along the marked lines. Use pins to hold the curve of the string until the glue dries.

4 Assemble the box using the nails and no glue (so that it can be taken apart later). Cover the square of MDF with clear plastic wrap and insert into the base of the box.

5 To make the concrete, combine one part cement with seven parts sharp sand in a suitable container. I made use of one of the plastic cups used in the project to measure out the quantities, and needed two cups of cement and fourteen cups of sand.

6 Add water and mix the concrete until it becomes a thick liquid that finds its own level in the mixing container. Tap the container several times to get air bubbles to rise to the surface. The concrete will not set properly if it contains any air.

7 Pour the concrete into the mold and gently tap the sides to level the mixture. Measure the length of one of the candles against one of the plastic cups to check how deep it needs to be sunk, and then push the cups into the wet concrete.

8 Check the cups are level with each other and evenly spaced, and fill them with sand. Then leave the mold to dry for several days.

9 Tip out the sand and remove the base. Push down on the sides of the cups to release the airlock and then pull out.

10 Carefully ease the wooden sides of the box apart. Pull off the pieces of string to reveal the indented wave design. If the concrete is still crumbly, stop and leave it overnight to dry off some more.

11 Insert the candles into the holes. If the holes are too deep, you can raise the height of the candles as required using a layer of sand.

12 Because it is made of concrete, it is safe to use your candle holder on any surface, but make sure that it is scratch-resistant. As with all candles, do not leave unattended while alight.

bamboo

For many of us, bamboo is simply the thin cane we use for supporting plants in the garden, but there is much more to this very versatile material. For the Japanese, bamboo is a mystical plant, symbolizing strength, flexibility, tenacity, endurance, and compromise. It grows faster than any other woody plant, making it one of Japan's most valuable natural resources. As there are over one thousand species of bamboo in the world, ranging from miniature varieties to the giant plants that grow up to 100 feet (60 meters) tall, it is available to us in a wide variety of shapes and sizes.

Bamboo brings an instant oriental feel to a home. It can be used to

make all sorts of decorative utensils cutting pieces to length and tying bamboo and carefully secured the make the base for an elegant glass-green because it is still fresh; the months to the more familiar pale

Because it is a natural plant, top to bottom. I used this natural bamboo for the towel rail and the

and low, angular furniture, by simply them together. I chose wide green pieces with natural seagrass to topped coffee table. The bamboo is color will gradually fade over a few golden color.

longer lengths of bamboo taper from shaping when cutting lengths of shoe rack, where the narrower top

shelf uses the thin end of the bamboo. To retain the natural look, use materials such as raffia or seagrass twine to tie the bamboo together.

Bamboo can split if it dries out too much and so is an ideal material to use in the bathroom where the moist atmosphere helps to keep it in perfect condition. The natural appearance of bamboo accessories such as the towel rail and soap dish will coordinate with any color scheme.

BAMBOO

coffee
table

Glass is often used to make low tables in modern Japanese homes. Japanese people are such avid collectors of unusual and interesting artifacts that all kinds of objects can be used for a base: anything from a giant porcelain urn to an antique chest. The glass gives the impression that dishes or ornaments placed on the table are floating above the floor, and it complements perfectly the beautiful green bamboo used as a base.

"Green" bamboo is bamboo that is freshly cut and still has its original color. It is kept refrigerated to preserve the color and is available from flower markets. The bamboo will dry out and slowly change to the more familiar golden hue over several months. Cut the pieces of bamboo to the exact height of the table required and then tie together. I used seagrass, which is a natural pale green twine usually used for covering chair seats. The base needs to be tied together at intervals down the bamboo to make it stable. Work around the base, tightening the seagrass again before tying the ends in a secure knot. The tabletop is stenciled with a Japanese calligraphy motif, using frosting glaze to give the appearance of etched glass.

The glass tabletop allows you to appreciate the sculptural quality of the green bamboo and the richly contrasting texture of the tied seagrass.

JAPAN

JAPAN

Green bamboo is slightly more difficult to cut than dry bamboo.
To avoid ragged edges, work around the bamboo, cutting just into the outer skin,
and then cut straight through.

MATERIALS

- *Approximately 20ft/6m bamboo*
3¹⁄₂in/9cm wide
- *Miter saw*
- *1lb/¹⁄₂kg seagrass*
- *29¹⁄₂in/75cm diameter circular piece*
toughened glass ¹⁄₄in/6mm thick
- *Denatured alcohol*
- *Japanese letter stencil*
- *Spray mount*
- *Frosting glaze*
- *Stencil brush*

Finished size of tabletop: 29¹⁄₂in/75cm
diameter; height: 16in/41cm.

1 Cut the bamboo into sixteen 16in/41cm lengths with a miter saw so that the ends are absolutely straight. Make sure that the pieces are all exactly the same length by using the saw's gauge.

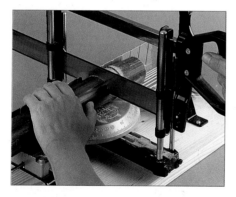

A Japanese symbol is stippled onto the glass tabletop using a traditional stencil and frosting glaze, forming a delicate contrast to the strong lines of the green bamboo base.

2 Lay the pieces side by side and tie them together. Begin in the middle of a 10ft/3m length of seagrass. Loop around the first piece and then cross the ends over on the other side. Add the next piece and cross the ends of the seagrass on the other side again. Keep adding pieces of bamboo in this way.

3 Wrap three or four new 10ft/3m lengths of seagrass along the bamboo, spaced out along the length of the pieces. Lift the bamboo up to form a circle. Thread each end of the seagrass into the opposite loop and tie the ends loosely. Tighten the seagrass around each piece of bamboo before tying off the ends securely.

4 Test to see if the tabletop fits stably onto the bamboo base. If it is rickety, add further rows of seagrass at the top and bottom of the bamboo and tighten before tying off.

5 Measure and mark the center of the glass tabletop. Turn it face down and then clean the underside with denatured alcohol. Allow to dry.

6 Spray the right side of the stencil with spray mount and position in the center of the glass tabletop.

7 Put a little of the frosting glaze in the lid of the jar. Pick up a little of the glaze on the stencil brush and stipple the motif onto the glass. Keep stippling until the glaze is thinly and evenly spread. Allow to dry.

8 Arrange the bamboo base upright on the floor and lift the glass tabletop into position. The finished table is sturdy enough to use as a coffee table.

shoe rack

The entrance of a Japanese house sets the mood for the rest of it. The hallway or *Genkan* is known as the "face" of the house. It is a space set aside to ease the transition from the hustle and bustle of the outside world to the more tranquil and private surroundings of home. The hallway introduces the ambience and style of the interior. There is usually an arrangement of flowers, an interesting collection of artifacts, or an exquisite piece of furniture like this unusual shoe rack, to define the taste and style of the owners of the house.

As it is the custom in Japan for family and visitors to change their shoes outside the door or in the hallway before going into the house, this bamboo shoe rack is the ideal way to keep an orderly appearance. There is plenty of room for half a dozen pairs of shoes, and the narrower upper shelf is just the right size for smaller children's shoes. You can increase the length to suit your requirements.

Natural raffia is used to tie the pieces of bamboo together. The cross straps at the back of the shoe rack make the design remarkably sturdy.

JAPAN

Because bamboo poles are smooth, sticking double-sided tape around the bamboo before tying with raffia will make the structure much stronger and less likely to pull apart.

MATERIALS

- *Bamboo—approximately 18yd/18m of ¾in/18mm diameter*
- *Pencil*
- *Hacksaw or miter saw*
- *Sanding block*
- *Masking tape*
- *Double-sided tape*
- *1 small bundle raffia*
- *T-square*
- *Tape measure*

Finished size: 31½ x 23¾ x 15¼in/ 80 x 60 x 40cm

1 Cut the following lengths from bamboo: *framework:* one 31½in/80cm, four 28¼in/72cm, two 23½in/60cm; *shelf supports:* two 15in/38cm, two 10in/25cm; *shelves:* eight 31½in/80cm of wider bamboo, twelve 31½in/80cm of narrower bamboo.

2 Sand the ends of the poles to remove any rough edges.

3 Arrange the pieces for the back of the frame on a flat surface. Begin by placing the 23½in/60cm uprights about 31½in/80cm apart. Lay the 31½in/80cm framework piece in position across the top. Carefully secure all the joints with thin strips of masking tape.

The bamboo poles are secured with double-sided sticky tape and then lashed together with raffia at each joint of the shoe rack.

4 Arrange the two narrowest 28¼in/72cm lengths in an inverted V-shape, crossing over at the top. Place one piece behind the crossbar and one in front, and securely tape around the joint.

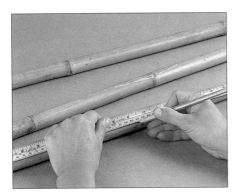

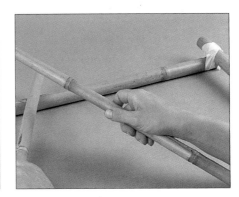

5 Carefully lift up the frame and lean it against a wall. Attach a 28¼in/72cm length of bamboo to each inside edge of the joints on the top bar with masking tape, and create the diagonal sides of the shoe rack by pulling them forwards and taping them temporarily to the work surface to make them rigid. Insert the longer (15in/38cm) shelf supports horizontally into each joint at the lower back of the framework, remove the tape holding them to the work surface, and tape the other ends to the diagonal sections. Once they are in place, check that the supports are level with the work surface.

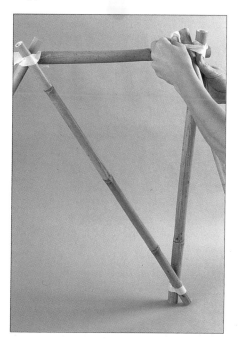

6 Lay the eight wider 31½in/80cm shelf poles onto the lower shelf supports. Adjust the position of the shoe rack's framework, if required, so that the poles protrude no further than just outside the frame and fit snugly together to form a sturdy shelf. (*see picture next column*)

7 Tape the shorter shelf supports as far down from the top as possible on the side panels, adjusting the height so that the eight narrower poles fit neatly to form a shelf. The tapered poles will fit together more neatly if arranged nose to tail.

8 Remove one piece of tape at a time, in the order that the frame was built, and wrap each joint with double-sided tape.

9 Wrap each joint tightly with raffia—the double-sided tape you have already applied should stop the raffia slipping against the shiny bamboo poles. It may help at this stage if you enlist a friend to hold the poles in place while you bind the joints.

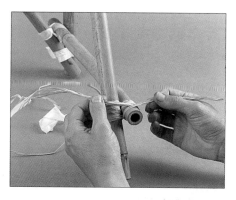

10 Use a T-square to check that the back panel of the framework is at a right-angle to the work surface, and a tape measure to check that all the shelves are level.

11 Lift out the shelf poles.

12 Re-fit the shelf poles one at a time by binding with raffia. Begin at the back, in the middle of a length of raffia, and wrap both ends over the pole and under the shelf support each time.

towel rail

Bathrooms present a wonderful opportunity for the application of Japanese style. Simple tiled walls and a plain wood floor provide an ideal backdrop for a few well-chosen accessories. In Japan, display is a fine art. Interesting objects, often antiques found after much searching in flea markets, are arranged with meticulous care. Accessories are usually selected for their color, shape, or texture and then grouped to show each to its best advantage. In the bathroom, choose soft white towels to contrast with the smooth golden surface of the bamboo towel rail.

This bamboo towel rail was inspired by the antique "scholar's ladders" used to reach books on high shelves. The wide base and narrow top make it fairly stable and easy to balance against a wall. The ladder can be made as tall as you like, as bamboo can be bought in a variety of lengths up to 10 feet (3 meters). Graduate the space between the rungs, with the gap narrowing towards the top.

▶ 101

The warm honey hues of natural bamboo work effortlessly with any bathroom color scheme, yet make an interesting contrast to the white waffle towels and bathrobe.

The rungs on this bamboo ladder are spaced so that the gap between the two outer poles gradually increases between the top and the bottom rungs. The top rungs are about 9in/23cm apart, and the bottom rungs 12in/30cm apart.

KNOWLEDGE OF POWER TOOLS REQUIRED

MATERIALS
◆ *Two 5ft/150cm lengths 1³⁄₈in/3.5cm diameter bamboo*
◆ *Hacksaw or miter saw*
◆ *Pencil*
◆ *Tape measure*
◆ *One 5ft/150cm length ⁵⁄₈in/1.5cm diameter bamboo*
◆ *Drill and hole drill bit*
◆ *Clear varnish*

Finished size: width 20in/51cm at base, 10in/25cm at top; height 55in/140cm

1 For the main poles, choose two similar-looking pieces of bamboo and check that they are not cracked or look likely to split. Cut them about 55in/140cm long. A miter saw set at right angles will hold and cut the bamboo exactly square.

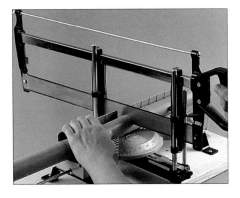

2 Mark the positions of the rungs of the ladder approximately 12in/30cm apart, on the two thicker bamboo poles.

3 Position the mark for the first rung about 6in/15cm from the top and the last 12in/30cm from the bottom.

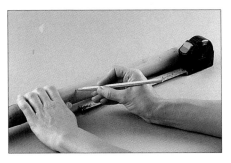

4 Lay the bamboo poles out on a flat surface so that the tops are 10in/25cm apart and the bottom ends 20in/50cm apart. Cut pieces of narrower bamboo to fit between the marks as rungs, allowing ³⁄₈–³⁄₄in/1–2cm at each end to fit inside the poles.

5 Measure the diameter of the ends of the rungs and choose a drill bit the same size. Drill holes for the rungs into the main poles, in careful straight lines.

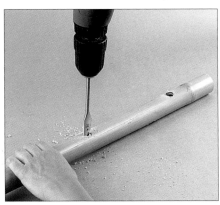

6 Check the size of the rung against the hole you have drilled for it, and file with a round file if required until the rung fits snugly inside. Don't force the rung into too tight a hole, as this will cause the thicker bamboo to split. If a rung turns out to be too narrow for its hole, try binding the end of it with thread before inserting it.

7 Fit the rungs into one side of the ladder, then line up the other side and tap the rungs gently into place with your fist.

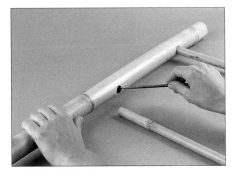

8 If you wish, paint the towel rail with clear varnish to protect it and make it glossy. Standing the ladder at an angle to your bathroom wall allows the towels to hang separately and dry overnight.

Use two stout bamboo poles for the two main supports of the towel rail, and narrower lengths of bamboo for the rungs.

BAMBOO

soap dish

One of the unique aspects of Japanese culture is the ritual of bathing. Traditionally the body is scrubbed and cleansed before the person enters the bath, then a soak in warm water encourages rejuvenation and complete relaxation. The Japanese bath is traditionally wooden and all the accoutrements in the bathroom are made from natural materials such as reed, rattan, and bamboo in order to create a restful and tranquil atmosphere. We can adopt some of these Japanese elements in our own bathroom accessories, so as to achieve a similar ambience.

This simple soap dish has been made from a piece of bamboo cut in half and the two halves pinned together using bamboo skewers. The natural curved surface of the bamboo is the ideal shape for keeping a bar of soap in perfect condition, as there is always a channel under the bar to allow the soap to dry. This dish also has drainage holes to let any water run away.

The sculptural quality of the soap dish enhances the simplest bathroom décor. Complement it with a bar of your favorite soap.

The outside skin of bamboo is quite tough: you may find it easier to use an electric sander to sand the two curved edges so that the sections fit together successfully.

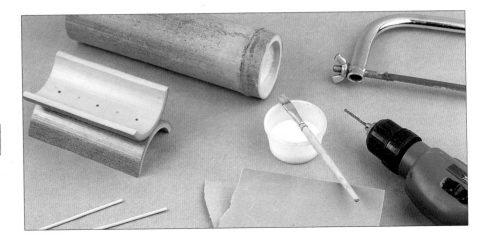

KNOWLEDGE OF POWER TOOLS REQUIRED

MATERIALS
◆ 6in/15cm piece 3in/10cm diameter bamboo
◆ Band-, miter, or hacksaw
◆ Sanding block
◆ Drill and drill bit
◆ Wood glue
◆ Bamboo skewer
◆ Craft knife

Finished size: 6 x 3in/15.5 x 7.5cm

1 Sand the ends of the bamboo and mark the center of the round end. Cut it in half lengthwise using a fine tooth bandsaw, hacksaw, or miter saw (which will make the edges exactly straight) to make the two halves of the soap dish.

2 Sand along the straight edges and the bottom curves so that the two pieces lie closer together. (see picture next column)

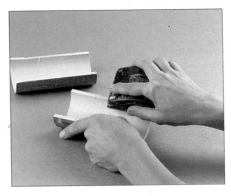

3 Mark five holes, evenly spaced, along the center of the top piece of bamboo. Drill through the top piece only, then position the sections together and drill through the stand.

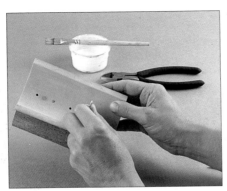

4 Spread a thin layer of glue along the curved edges of the two halves. Fit the two glued surfaces together and hold them firmly. It may help to bind them with string temporarily to ensure a snug fit. Drop a little glue into the two outside holes and the middle holes.

5 With a craft knife, cut three neat bamboo skewers, about 7/8in/2cm long. Push the skewers into the holes until the ends are flush with the top surface of the soap dish.

6 Allow the glue to dry and then cut off the excess on the underside with the craft knife.

106 ◀

t e m p l a t e s

sashiko table mats
actual size

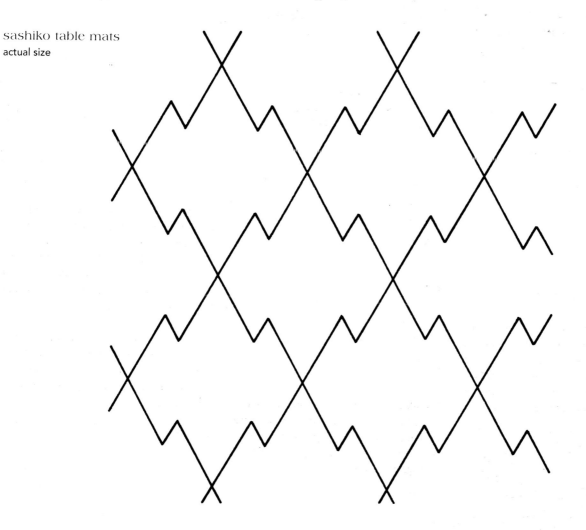

floor cushions
diagram for Turk's head knot

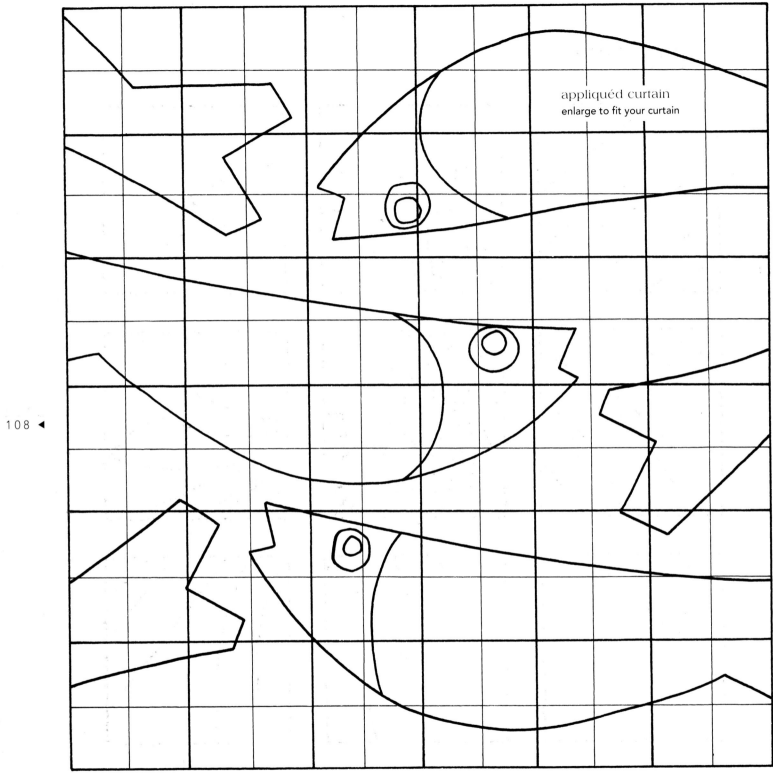

appliquéd curtain
enlarge to fit your curtain

JAPAN

paneled paper hanging
enlarge as required

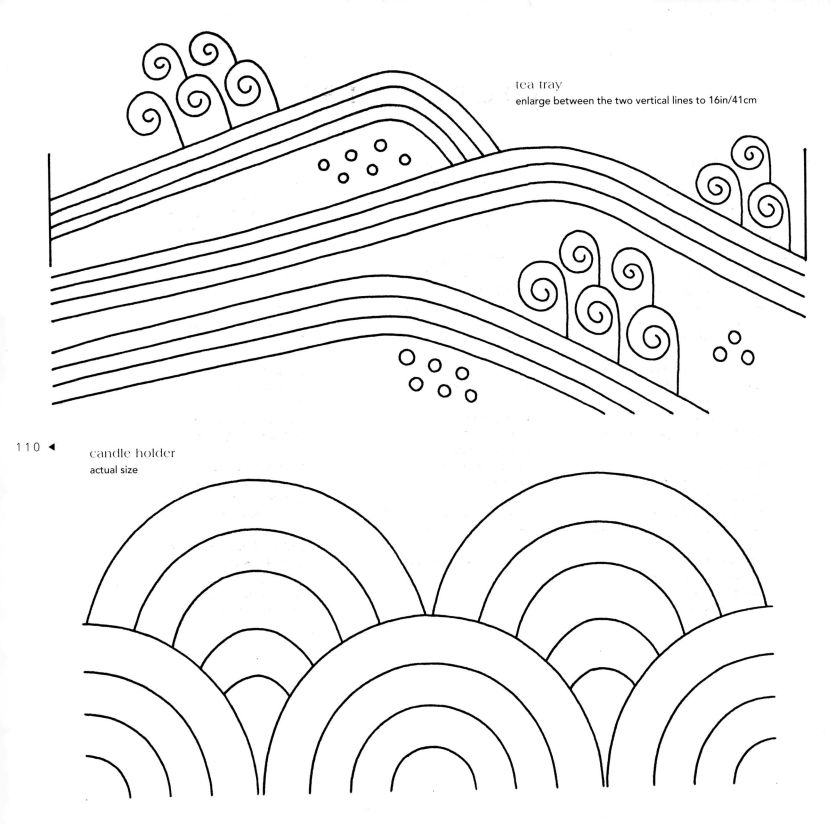

tea tray
enlarge between the two vertical lines to 16in/41cm

110 ◄

candle holder
actual size

source list

The Art Store
Los Angeles, California
www.artstore.com
(323) 933-9284
Call for other store locations
Art and craft supplies

Ace Hardware
Rockland, California
(916) 632-2200
Call for other store locations
General hardware

Baron's Fabrics & Sewing Centers
Woodland Hills, California
(818) 348-7012
www.baronsewfab.com
Fabrics, sewing supplies, notions

Britex Fabrics
San Francisco, California
(415) 392-2910
www.britexfabrics.com
Fabrics, sewing supplies, notions

Cane and Basket
Los Angeles, California
(323) 939-9644
Assorted canes

Curry's Art Supplies
Mississauga, Ontario
(905) 272-4460
Call for other store locations
Craft and design supplies

Flax Art & Design
San Francisco, California
(800) 547-7778
Papers, art and craft supplies

Hiromi Paper International
Santa Monica, CA
(310) 998-0098
Handmade Japanese papers

Home Depot
(800) 430-3376
www.homedepot.com
Call for store locations
Hardware, woods

Janovic/Plaza Inc.
Long Island City, New York
(800) 722-4381
Specialty decorating supplies

Jo-Ann Fabrics and Crafts
Hudson, Ohio
(330) 656-2600
Call for other store locations
*Fabrics, sewing supplies,
art and craft supplies*

Kate's Paperie
New York City, New York
(212) 941-9816
www.katespaperie.com
Fine papers

Michael's
(800) MICHAELS
www.michaels.com
Call for store locations
Craft and hobby supplies

Needlepoint, Inc.
San Francisco, California
(415) 392-1622
Assorted threads

Orchard Supply Hardware
(888) SHOP-OSH
www.osh.com
Call for store locations
Hardware, wood

▶ 111

index